Discovering Jesus

Awakening to God

By Gerrit Scott Dawson

REFORMATION PRESS

Discovering Jesus: Awakening To God
© 2007 by Gerrit Scott Dawson

Reformation Press books, monographs and other resources are available at special discounts in bulk purchases for educational and ministry use. For more details, contact:

Director of Publications
Reformation Press
136 Tremont Park Drive
Lenoir, North Carolina 28645

Call us at 1-800-368-0110
Or Visit Reformation Press on the Web at www.resourcecatalog.org

Cover Design: Joel McClure/HeuleGordon, Inc.; Grand Rapids, Michigan

Printed in the United States of America

Discovering Jesus

Awakening to God

By Gerrit Scott Dawson

For Mary-Emeline

Who Loves to Discover God
Again and Again in His Word

TABLE OF CONTENTS

Introduction

As a pastor, I hear from people who feel far from God. As a Christian, my deepest joy is knowing God intimately and personally through his Son, Jesus Christ. So, I want to help them make the connection. I love to help people find the way back to their home in God.

Fourteen years ago, my heart was so tugged by the people who shared their yearning for God that I wrote my first book, *Heartfelt: Finding Our Way Back to God*. It was an attempt to help people get close to God through meeting Jesus in the stories of the gospels.

Since then, I have talked to a lot more people. I have done a lot more reading in the Scriptures and a lot more thinking. I am more convinced than ever that God will meet those who seek him through his Word. It is my privilege to attempt to serve as the one making the introductions.

Chapter One explores the kind of quest we will be on to find God in the place he has said he could be found. Then, the next 11 chapters involve actually meeting God through a dozen accounts from the New Testament about what Jesus said and did.

I am grateful that Reformation Press has published this completely revised and expanded edition of *Heartfelt*, now titled, *Discovering Jesus: Awakening to God*.

I pray that you will draw closer to God by working through this book – on your own or, even better, in a group of fellow seekers. I would be delighted to be in correspondence with you concerning your questions and thoughts. I'd also love to hear of your experiences in studying these passages.

May the presence of Jesus fill you with joy as you meet him in the gospels!

Gerrit Scott Dawson
Fairlight Cottage
Brevard, North Carolina
Christmas 2006
Gerrit@fpcbr.org

xiii

Ten Tips for Leaders

Using Discovering Jesus *in Groups*

After each chapter, there are questions and exercises to help you go deeper into the stories and the connection to your own life. Of course, you can do this work on your own, but the book is designed for small group study.

I suggest this plan of action:

1. Gather six-to-12 people willing to undertake this study with you. You can commit to the whole 13 weeks of studying the entire book, or begin with a seven-week study of just the first half.
2. Ask group members to read the chapter to be discussed prior to your meeting.
3. Meet weekly in a home for about 90 minutes. The study itself should be allotted an hour, with the rest for gathering, coffee, prayer and sharing.
4. Be sure to begin the first week taking time for introductions and getting to know each other a bit before plunging ahead. Chapter One is shorter than the others to allow for this time. If people don't receive their books until the first session, you may want to read Chapter One aloud to begin.
5. Begin each session with prayer that Jesus would meet you in this very hour through the Scripture you are studying. Ask him to connect each of you to God in a fresh, real way.
6. Read aloud the Scripture passage on which the chapter is based.
7. Work through the questions provided. Encourage discussion and application to individual lives. Supplement the discussion-starter questions as needed.
8. During the discussion, re-read aloud any portions of the chapter that you have highlighted and find appropriate for discussing further.
9. Invite group members to complete one or more of the exercises suggested or others that you create. Share the responses in the group.
10. Leave plenty of time to pray for one another before you close. Invite prayer requests of any nature, but also be sure to pray for one another's quest to meet God through a personal encounter with Jesus.

Chapter 1

IS THIS YOU?

I want to get connected to God.
But.
But I don't know how.
I don't even know how God feels about connecting to *me*.
In fact, I suspect God doesn't feel too great about where I am in my life.

What makes me happy probably doesn't please God very much. Maybe a lot of what I like to do, say, buy, eat, drink and think is just what God wants me to get rid of. So, sometimes I figure that if there is *more of God* in my life, there will be *less of me*.

I'm not sure I do want to get connected to God after all!

Still.

There's got to be more to life than I'm experiencing. I'm not satisfied even after I get what I thought would fill me with pleasure.

Something is always missing.

I've got questions I can't answer:

Am I more than just an insignificant speck in the cosmos? Am I ultimately just alone in myself? I want to know if I can be connected to something more, to *Someone* beyond me who gives meaning to life. I want to feel known deep in my bones.

Is there more life to come or is now all there is? I want to know if the people I have lost are gone forever or if I will see them again. I want to know if I will live after I die. And, if so, will that be a good thing? How can I get in on it?

Am I OK? Actually, I want to know how I can feel OK about myself again, for I know that something is not right. I'm not sure I'm measuring up. In fact, I've done some damage. I've failed people. I've done wrong and I don't know how to get rid of the guilt. Rationalizing doesn't work. Neither does comparing myself to others. Neither does working harder and doing more. How can I feel right again?

Is there a point? A bigger picture? The goals and dreams of our culture are not enough. I want to live for something higher than myself – something that will give me a sense of real worth and a passionate purpose. I want to feel that my life counts for something.

What's the matter with the world? Aren't things supposed to be better than this?

I know the question is a cliché, but it still haunts me: "Why do bad things keep happening to good people?" I want to know what the plan is to fix this mess – to end the violence, lift up the poor, save the earth and help people get along.

I suspect that the answers to all these questions have to do with discovering Jesus.

So, yes, actually I *do* want to get connected to God – even if I have to risk losing something of myself. Because what I am isn't working. There's got to be more.

I want to find the way back to God.

But I don't know how.

You're Normal!

If you saw yourself in any of that description, then welcome to the club. You're one of us who have come awake to our need for God. We know he's there and that our lives depend on connecting to him. We want real life. We want a significant life. We want to come alive with the presence of God that heals us, fills us, enthuses us and sends us into our days with a magnificent purpose. Through God, we want to find relationships with other people that are deep, honest, joyous and lasting. We want to be part of making this sad world a better place. We want the real deal with God.

But we have some very natural fears of what God will be like should we turn to him. A lot of it is based on bad information. We may have equated keeping petty rules with pleasing God. We can mistakenly come to think that anything that feels like life is what God opposes. So, anything that puts us in a legalistic straight-jacket of rules-keeping must be what he wants. We may have gone to particular churches and decided (quite rightly!) that if being with God is like *that*, we'd better find a different way as soon as possible. But then, once we've broken enough rules, we may feel we're so far gone that there's just no way back to a holy God. So, we fear what will happen should we return to him.

Or, we can get bad information that goes the other way. We may have heard that God is a mystery. God has many faces that he shows to the world at different times and in different ways. There are many paths to this hidden God, and we each have to find the one that's right for us. In American culture, the God we most often choose is the God who is happy when we're happy. This is the God who helps us fulfill our dreams. He is with us as we struggle to live the lives we've chosen for ourselves. He is tolerant and kindly. He does not meddle too much.

The problem, of course, arises when our own choices inevitably fail to fulfill us. If God is merely a supportive presence while we direct our lives, then such a God is powerless to be of any real help when we are overwhelmed. He may feel for us, but this God just leaves it up to us to solve our messes. We are left stuck in ourselves, mired in the questions we cannot answer and the situations we cannot solve. Why read a book on awakening to God if God is just an extension of ourselves?

> *We want the real deal with God. … We crave a God who knows us utterly, loves us passionately and transforms us continually.*

Yet, if you've read these few pages, you have dared to hope that the real God is more than an angry rule-giver or some benign force of positivity. Our hearts long for:

+ A God who is both personal and powerful, accepting and yet demanding that we be more than mediocre.
+ A God who knows us utterly, loves us passionately, and transforms us continually.
+ A God whose heart and mind, will and way, can be truly known by his children, even though we could never fully grasp all of who he is.
+ A God who has truly acted in his world, who is working now and will bring even more to pass in the future.
+ A God who is ardently interested in the tiniest details of our lives, even as he calls us into a life of higher purpose than our own pursuits.
+ A God who gives us true freedom so that our choices really matter, but who also has a plan for transforming the mess we've made of things in our freedom.
+ A God who forgives in a way that truly washes clean our guilt.
+ A God who can answer the riddle of death with eternal life.
+ A God who addresses the evil in the world with radical love.

I believe we are made to be in communion with such a God as this. Knowing him, we do not lose our distinctive selves. Rather, we find our lives – our truest selves, what we were made to be – when we are united to him.

19

Come With Me

You can find the way to this God, because he is eager to show you. I believe your life can be transformed as you reconnect with God, because the real God desires to connect you to himself. He seeks you. He is working even now to overcome your hesitancy and resistance with his love. If you ask him, he will come to you. If you seek him in the place where he gives himself to be known, you will find him. If you knock for admittance to God's presence, he will open the door to you.

This is how it works. Indeed, God has opened a way for us to get connected to him. He has provided the terms for our being joined to him. He has provided a place where we may encounter him:

The path to God leads through a personal encounter with Jesus Christ.

It is just that simple and just that demanding. God has made his true heart known to us in Jesus. The man Jesus of Nazareth is actually the eternal Son of God who came among us in flesh and blood. Jesus, as the God who became man and the man who is God, is the meeting place between us and God. The purposes of God for restoring a broken world are being worked out through his Son Jesus. So, to get reconnected with God and his work, we have to enter a personal, dynamic relationship with Jesus Christ.

But how do we have an encounter with someone who lived 2,000 years ago?

This is where the miracle comes in. This is what makes Christianity different from every other religion. This is what makes me know that in Christ I am encountering the real God. Jesus meets us *today* through the words of the New Testament written so long ago. It works like this:

We *ask* Jesus to meet us in his Word, to make the words of the Bible words to us right now. Then we read the stories of what Jesus did. We *hear* the words he spoke to people and the parables he told to the crowds. Alone or in a group, we approach Jesus with both the request and the expectation (sometimes feeble and full of doubt) that his Word will be real to us. Next, we start *considering* these interactions Jesus had with people. What was going on in their lives? How are their feelings and circumstances similar to ours? In the midst of this work, we enter a communion that joins us to every disciple who ever lived and unites us to Christ himself. We find that Jesus is addressing us as freshly and powerfully as when he spoke 2,000 years ago.

How can this be so?

The answer may sound incredible to you. It may be more than you can accept. But I invite you to try it on, to experiment with the possibility as you read through these chapters. We can meet Jesus today - first, because Jesus himself is alive right now. Unlike the founders of any other religion, Jesus is not buried somewhere in the ground. He is risen from the dead and alive in heaven right now. Second, Jesus sends us his Holy Spirit from heaven. The Spirit opens our hearts so Christ's words to others become words truly addressed to us. He causes us to understand what Jesus said and did. He joins us to Jesus in such a way that the very life of Jesus comes to live within our lives. So, the Spirit makes the risen Jesus to be as real to us *now* as he was to the first disciples back then!

> *Jesus meets us today, right where we are, as we make the gospel stories our own.*

Now, this is a great mystery, but it is not magic. It doesn't happen in the blink of an eye. We go to the place where God has given himself to be known. *We go to the Scriptures.* We read the stories about Jesus and the stories he told to his disciples. We enter those stories by connecting to the people we meet there. We consider how we are like them, how we share their feelings and circumstances, their needs and their hopes. Then we invite Jesus to deal with us as he dealt with them. And he does. Jesus by his Spirit meets us today, right where we are, as we make the gospel stories our own. During the days of his ministry, Jesus connected people to God. He still connects us to God today.

This path is not easy. But it is real. And as you walk along it, you will be reconnected to God and your life will be transformed. God has promised that this is the way he will meet us.

I invite you to come with me as we take up a dozen stories and parables of Jesus. I will do my best to provide you with points of entry into the stories. I will offer what I know of the insights into the characters, and point out guideposts along the way. We will think through how it is that Jesus has opened a new and living way to God.

But the work ultimately has to be yours. I encourage you to read the actual Bible passages that underlie each chapter. Ask God to connect you to himself as you study. Pray that his will would be done in your life. Ask him to meet you in the gospels. Then watch how he answers those prayers!

Questions for Reflection or Discussion

The Scriptures on which this chapter is based include: Hebrews 11:6; Jeremiah 29: 13-14; Matthew 7: 7; John 14: 25-26; Luke 24: 32-45.

The group leader should read aloud Jeremiah 29:13-14: "You will seek me and find me. When you seek me with all your heart, I will be found by you, declares the LORD."

- Consider the sentence, "I worry that if there is more of God in my life, there will be less of me." Why do you suppose so many people feel that way? What is it about God that we fear will diminish us?

- What questions would you add to the list of "unanswerables" given on pages 15-16?

- What kind of bad information do you feel you have received in the past about God? Another way to consider this is to ask, "How do you hope the real God does **not** turn out to be?"

- Read through the list on page 17 of the God our hearts yearn for. With which descriptions do you resonate? Can you say why? What other characteristics in God do you hope turn out to be true?

- Take a spiritual plus: How do you feel right now about the claim that God meets us through a personal encounter with Jesus in the Scriptures?

- This chapter asserts that the reason Jesus can be as real to us now as he was to his first followers is: a) because Jesus is risen from the dead and alive today; and b) because the Holy Spirit of God unites us to Jesus through the Word. What is your reaction to these two claims?

Exercises

Work through the two exercises below and discuss in your group as people feel comfortable.

- Individually, make a list of the things that make you hesitant to pursue a closer relationship with God.

- Individually, make a list of the reasons you feel motivated to pursue a closer relationship with God.

Chapter 2

WATCHING FOR OUR RETURN

Luke 15:11-24

We begin with a story Jesus told about two brothers and their father. This is one of the most famous teachings of Jesus, commonly called the Parable of the Prodigal Son. This story is the third in a series Jesus told about the ways God looks for us when we are lost and far from home.

Jesus began, "There was a man who had two sons. And the younger of them said to his father, 'Father, give me the share of property that is coming to me.' And he divided his property between them. Not many days later, the younger son gathered all he had and took a journey into a far country, and there he squandered his property in reckless living."

The younger son left home. In itself, that could have been just a normal part of growing up. After all, we cannot be children forever – at some point, we have to make our own way. But this man left by burning his bridges. According to the custom of the day, asking for his inheritance while his father still lived was like saying, "Father, I wish you were already dead." The son repudiated his heritage. He disgraced his family. He left all that he had been taught was good and right.

Now, the turning point in the story occurs after his money had run out and an economic depression hit the country. The young man took a job feeding pigs, animals repulsive to a Jewish man because they were "unclean." Yet, he grew so hungry that even the foul pig pods looked appetizing. His need became desperate. Finally, as Jesus told the story, the son "came to himself." Jesus' wonderfully succinct phrase implies that somehow the man had gone away from himself. He had started on a course of life and could not stop until he ran out of resources. When everything was gone, he "came to." He bottomed out and woke up. He returned to who he really was.

Waking Up Hungry

Sometimes, without even knowing it, we get ourselves on a road away from God and, therefore, away from our true selves. We may not even know how far away we are until "the money runs out." We have run through whatever we have been living on, and now our hearts growl with hunger. These pangs we experience vary in intensity:

> *We have run through whatever we have been living for and now our hearts growl with hunger.*

We may feel vaguely that life is just not what we thought it would be. We always had planned for something different. There's nothing particularly wrong. It's just that we thought we were supposed to feel more alive, experience more joy, be more enthused about living. We may have seen in our parents or grandparents a sense of tranquility about their place in the world. But that hasn't happened to us. We don't yet feel right in our own skin.

Or we may "come to" with a sickening sense of emptiness. The years have blown by. We hardly paid attention. Looking back, nothing stands out as significant. So little accomplished at work. So little love given to the world, to friends or even to family.

Worse still, we may wake up one day to an awful self-loathing. Life seems to have had no higher purpose than our immediate wants and comforts. We used people for our wants. Some we ran over, others we deceived, many more we ignored. There are no good grounds to justify our existence. And, increasingly, there is evidence that we have done more harm than good with the years given to us.

All the consuming we have done has not filled us. We stuff the need according to our tastes and economic ability: extreme sports or fine restaurants, remodeled kitchens or rebuilt engines, new titles at work to make us more powerful or new clothes to make us more attractive, a more daring deal or the perfect vacation. But when the "new" wears off, when what has occupied our attention runs out, the hunger roars back upon us. No matter what we do or get, we realize when we wake up to the condition of our lives that we are far from home.

At first, we may not be able to describe this *home*; we simply know we are not there. We may not know in those waking moments what being ourselves is supposed to be, but we feel sure that we have not been living in harmony with our innermost design. We may not have a description for what connecting with God could be like; we realize, however, that we are a long way from any such connection. Our need yanks us awake, and we begin to search for a way to get back.

In Jesus' story, the father who let the son go clearly represents God. This was consistent with the way Jesus taught his followers to call God "Our Father." Such intimacy was unprecedented. Jesus showed us the reality that God is the great Father for whom we have been longing. He is our source and protector, our guide and our goal. God, then, is intimately connected with all that makes up home.

> *The father is the source of blessing; his house is the place where life is in balance.*

The father in the story is the source of blessing; his house is the place where life is in balance. His presence is healing and safety. On his land is to be found the work that satisfies and generates an abundant harvest. In his sight is the affirmation we crave. If we would be at peace and at home with ourselves, we will have to be at home with God our Father – for the Father *is* home. But before we consider how we can return to God, we need to consider how we got so far from God in the first place.

The Impulse to Leave

Why did the younger son head off for the far country? Obviously, he didn't set out with the ultimate goal of becoming a professional pig feeder. He must have thought that what he wanted, what would truly satisfy him, lay in a place far from the home he always had known.

So, why have *we* sought our happiness apart from God? Why do we take off on paths that lead directly away from the Father of blessing? There seem to be many possibilities:

+ Some people never knew any better. Growing up, they hardly heard of God. What they did hear was confusing or even repellent. They have spent years groping blindly after what makes for life and peace.
+ Some were wounded by a parent or family member at an early age. God, especially the Father, seems untrustworthy in view of such damage. They feel on their own in this world.
+ Some say they left because they wanted to try their hand at the world's game. Our culture prizes the achievements of position and wealth. Such rewards

entice us to try and master the game, even at the risk of our souls. So often the world looks much more interesting than God (especially as God gets represented by some people in churches).

+ Some went in quest of the mysterious, to seek the rush of spiritual experience or passion in the arts. Those of a religious temperament may have left all they knew of God in search of God. They wanted a God who seemed more full-blooded than the thin religiosity taught them in their youth.

+ Others went off to fill up a sense of unworthiness. They left home to try to fill the expectations others had for them. One may have leaped into a marriage without reflection, and then tried awfully hard to portray a particular appearance. Another may have pursued someone else's measure of a successful life.

+ Still others may have given up trying to relate to God because of suffering a loss so searing that bitterness continues to block any possibility of faith.

+ Many of those raised in churches have left God because of how his people act. An experience of rejection or betrayal in the church led some to pack their bags and leave behind anything religious. A legalistic atmosphere can threaten to suck the life out of us. Some could not reason their way out of that trap, so they simply left faith behind.

There are thousands of reasons that send us away from home in God our Father. They involve seeking the goodness of God in sources other than God. Many lose their way for quite heartbreaking and even understandable reasons. But whether our flight to the far country seems warranted is not the real issue. The root cause is deeper than any presenting explanation. We all have believed a very ancient lie: that God does not have our best interests at heart. We can do better for ourselves when we live on our own rather than live in harmony with God. I want to be the master of my own life and I do not want any God imposing his will upon me. The truth is, I am as willing as the prodigal son to squander my Father's heritage to do what I want because I believe that what I want will be more fulfilling than what God wants for me. I do not trust that God will take care of me.

I do not believe that the Father is good.

The poet George Herbert knew well our urge to leave home and strike out on our own. He understood how our defiance can grow when we think there is something better for us in another place. In "The Collar," the poet expresses how he feels trapped by the expectations of his faith regarding what is right. So, he pounds the table and attempts to declare his independence. He is going to get what he wants before life passes him by, instead of wasting his life at home.

Herbert writes:

> I struck the board, and cried, No more.
> I will abroad.
> What? shall I ever sigh and pine?
> My lines and life are free; free as the road,
> Loose as the wind, as large as store.
> Shall I be still in suit?
> --------------------------------------
> Sure there was wine
> Before my sighs did dry it: there was corn
> Before my tears did drown it.
> Is the year only lost to me?
> Have I no bays to crown it?
> No flowers, no garlands gay? all blasted?
> All wasted?
> Not so, my heart: but there is fruit,
> And thou hast hands.[1]

Herbert hit the nerve of our impulse to wander. Something in us makes a bold declaration: "My life is free, free as the road, loose as the wind." I can live how I want to live, for my life is my own. There is fruit to be tasted in the world, and I have hands to pluck it down. I am going after it. Quietly or with a flash, brazenly or almost imperceptibly, we take a road away from our heart's home.

To Know that Someone Waits

When the son had come to himself, his pride was broken and he determined to go back to his father and ask for a job as a servant. The young man felt shame, but his need was stronger than his guilt. He prepared a speech of confession: "Father, I have sinned against heaven and before you; I am no longer worthy to be called your son. Treat me as one of your hired servants." So, taking these words of confession, the younger son got up and headed for home.

Jesus continued: "But while he was still a long way off, his father saw him and

---

1   Herbert, George; "The Collar;" in Dawson, Gerrit Scott; *Love Bade Me Welcome: Daily Readings with George Herbert* (Lenoir, N.C.; Glen Lorien Books; 1997) p. 175.

felt compassion, and ran and embraced him and kissed him." The son began his admission, but the father did not let him finish. He called for the finest robe and a ring representing family place and authority to be brought, along with shoes for his bruised and barefoot boy. The father ordered a great feast. "For this my son was dead, and is alive again; he was lost, and is found."

Suddenly, we learn that the father all along had been watching the road. The son had shamed him. By custom, the father could have repudiated the very existence of such a wanton child. Wasting time looking for his return made the father a subject of derision. But the father was crazy about his son; he loved him enough to cast his sight down the foreign road every day his child was away. When his son returned, he showered the shame with a welcome.

What would it mean to learn that someone is watching with straining eyes down the road to catch a glimpse of you? When we are far from home, what would happen if we realized that someone was waiting eagerly for the first signs of our return from a foreign land, waiting to celebrate our first steps home with open arms and a banquet of celebration?

> *Someone is waiting for me to come home!*

In the epilogue of Dostoyevsky's novel *Crime and Punishment*, we read of the beginning of renewal for the story's main character, Raskolnikov. Toward the beginning of the story, Raskolnikov had murdered an old woman pawnbroker, feeling no remorse and justifying his act as ridding society of an undesirable. Throughout the epic, he was wholly absorbed in himself – a narcissist fit for the 21st century.

Though Raskolnikov certainly is an unattractive character, one woman still loved him. Sonia even followed Raskolnikov all the way to the Siberian work camp, where he was sentenced to seven years of hard labor for his crime. She came to the fence every day to speak with him during brief breaks in the work.

For a long time, Raskolnikov spurned her presence. It meant nothing to him. He would remain quiet when he was with her, as if annoyed. Then, Raskolnikov fell ill and was placed in the hospital ward for many weeks.

Sonia tried to see him, but only rarely could gain admittance. Still, she came every day, "sometimes only to stand a minute and look up at the windows of the ward."

Raskolnikov's condition improved slowly. One evening he felt strong enough to rise from his bed and go to the window. He looked out and saw Sonia standing at the hospital gate; she appeared to be waiting for something. "Something stabbed him to the heart at that minute." He realized that every day he had been ill, unable to rise, believing himself alone in his misery, Sonia had come to the gate to wait awhile for him.

Raskolnikov looked for Sonia eagerly the next day. But she did not come, nor the next day. And, then, Raskolnikov understood that he was waiting for Sonia. Before, she had been the one waiting; now, he was the one. Before it had made no difference to him, but now he was expecting her. Before, he loathed her; now, he discovered that as he waited for her, he loved her.

When they met again at last, Raskolnikov found that "all at once something seemed to seize him and fling him at her feet. He wept and threw his arms around her knees." Sonia had out-waited his self-absorption until love broke through him at last. The one so far from home, in a Siberian prison and detached from his own soul, finally understood that someone had waited for him every day. He reconnected to life and came home to himself.[1]

There is one who waits for us. He stands every day in the yard looking up at the ward where we lie on a bed, mired in thoughts of our condition. He comes every day and stands in the cold winter light, and he waits while we think life is only this sick bed and the wants of our illness. He waits in the yard for the evening when we get up and look out the window to see him there – and our hearts are stabbed. Someone is waiting for us to come home! Our shame will not be answered with recrimination, but with tender forgiveness. He has not waited begrudgingly; he is not angry. This loving one has let go all the time that has gone by. He just wants us in his arms.

The father strained his eyes down the foreign road for any sign of his son. If we were to step into this story that Jesus told and began to consider that the Father was waiting for us now, would that be enough to get us to our feet? We may be able to slop the pigs in a foreign land for a long time if we do not believe there is any other choice, if shame prevents thoughts of home. But what yearning homeward is awakened when we discover that God our Father waits for us?

George Herbert concluded his poem of rebellion with these words:

> But as I raved and grew more fierce and wild
> At every word,
> Me thoughts I heard one calling, *Child:*
> And I replied, *My Lord.*

God, our loving heavenly Father, watches every moment for any sign of our

---

1   Dostoevsky, Fyodor; *Crime and Punishment* (New York, P.F. Collier & Son; 1917) Epilogue. With thanks for these insights to Vanstone, W.H.; *The Stature of Waiting* (London; Darton, Longman and Todd; 1982) pp. 96-8.

return. He is ready to embrace us even in our filth. He wants to love us through the shame and call us his own dear children!

The rest of this book is for those who feel the urge to get up and start down the road toward home in God.

Questions for Reflection or Discussion

Read aloud the story of the younger son as found in Luke 15:11-24.

+ What drives us to seize the inheritance, liquidate it, and strike out for a foreign country?
+ In what ways do you feel you have left home, in the sense that you feel away from your deepest self, away from God?
+ What feelings are evoked in you by the picture of the father with strained eyes looking down the road for signs of your return?
+ What resistance will you need to overcome before starting toward home?

Exercises

Work through some or all of the exercises below and then discuss as a group.

+ Jot down some words that describe the personality of the younger son, and also write some words that express his condition after the money runs out. Then, make a list of the words that come to mind when you think of the young man's father.
+ Imagine that you are the younger son (or daughter, if that makes it easier), longing to return. Prepare your homecoming speech. Allow your brief words to be a reflection on your life, and any ways in which you feel far from home.
+ Write a conversation between yourself as the younger child and the father who has awaited your return. Carry the story further by imagining what you talk about on the way back to the house. As the child, what feels important to say? How does the long-suffering parent, who is God, answer your concerns? Be sure to conclude your conversation with the father's words, "For this son (daughter) of mine was dead and is alive again; he (she) was lost and is found!"
+ The lines quoted above from George Herbert work well as a prayer.

Chapter 3

When Being Good Isn't Enough

Luke 15:25-32

The impulse to leave the Father's house to pursue life on our own terms is universal in the human heart. Of course, not everyone departs as dramatically as the younger son. Some of us stay home, like his older brother, and dutifully take care of our responsibilities. We have not had any major breaks with the values we received as children. Our parents rarely worried over us late at night. For the most part, we have maintained our faith in God, perhaps even serving in the church as part of our civic responsibility. Communities are built upon such people.

> *Elder brothers secretly feel that they are not worthy of God's love.*

Churches make pillars out of those who are like the older brother in Jesus' story. But such is human nature that good people can get estranged from home as well, without even leaving the premises.

When the younger son returned home, the father called for a feast. Almost immediately, there was music and dancing in the house. But there was still time left in the workday. The young man's older brother was out in the fields tending to the farm. As he got near the house, he heard the merriment and wondered what was going on. He asked a servant boy and was told, "Your brother has come, and your father has killed the fattened calf, because he has received him back safe and sound." As he thought about this, the elder brother got so angry that he refused to go to the party.

Shortly afterward, his father came out and pleaded with his son. But it did no good. The young man replied, "Look, these many years I have served you, and I never disobeyed your commands, yet you never gave me a young goat, that I might celebrate with my friends. But when this son of yours came, who has devoured your property with prostitutes, you killed the fattened calf for him!"

In the course of an hour, the father had gained one son, but had nearly lost the other one. Suddenly, it seemed that a happy, normal life all along had been a life of drudgery. Was this what it meant all these years? The elder brother perceived his life as working like a slave, obeying orders, slogging through each day in unexpressed hopes of some reward of distracting entertainment. He lived with his father and, yet, was as far away as a foreigner.

An Absence of Joy

The elder brother's sudden declaration of estrangement was extreme. In varying degrees of intensity, though, a number of us may experience this kind of distance from God. One common quality our faith may have with the older son is a dearth of joy. We find, perhaps, that we have no particular antipathy toward God; we simply have trouble getting deeper than the surface of religious practice. Some of us who go to church, say our prayers and try to live a good life nevertheless realize that if our faith stays small, our experience of God is negligible. Persisting in us is a quiet sense that, while others can connect with God, we do not. Others seem like they get it, and we may look like them; yet, we feel that, through some fault of our own, our spiritual life simply is not vital. Elder brothers secretly feel that they are not worthy of God's love.

Furthermore, resentment can build in us when the elder brother's sense of duty blocks our connection to the joy that is supposed to underlie all the work:

+ If we pray without experiencing the presence of God, before long the activity is mere empty habit.
+ Going to church regularly becomes drudgery when appearances before others replace warm fellowship.
+ We can scoff at the stories of the ways God transforms lives when it seems that only those who have been as prodigal as the younger brother receive rich experiences of grace. Aren't there any rewards for being good? Do you have to mess up your life and the lives of all those around you in order to know the joy of salvation?
+ We can burn out on mission work when there is no underlying spring replenishing our energies.
+ It is no joy at all to check our impulses and live a self-controlled, moral life if we have no sense of being part of a higher purpose by doing so.

So, faith can become just a chore. God can be but one more burden in a life of requirements. And being good simply isn't enough to restore our joy. Despite all we do, we never feel good *enough* to truly rejoice in the Father's presence. We may feel as lonely for God as if we'd gone to the far country.

Too Much Responsibility

Another quality we may share with the elder brother is a feeling of bondage to our responsibilities. The younger brother left without a thought toward how the family would get along maintaining the estate in his absence. The older son, though, never entertained thoughts of leaving for long. He knew that he was needed, and he lived in service to duty. This can happen today just as well.

For example, one child leaves town, makes her own way, gets married, and raises a family miles from home. Another child stays nearby and tends the family heritage. When the parents grow ill, the child at home takes on the burden. He feels he has no choice and, in fact, wouldn't want an alternative. But how it burns when that spendthrift sister can hardly manage a week away from her life to lend a hand!

Children who grow up in alcoholic families sometimes may find the same struggle, magnified to disastrous dimensions. One child seems to bear the weight of the family in her own body. It's her fault that Mom and Dad fight. Her father drinks because she – the unexpected, unwanted child – was born. She spends her life trying to fix things, trying to take control of the uncontrollable, shoveling her life into the bottomless hole of her parents' addiction. Is it any wonder she gets migraines no doctor can explain? She is the one who cleans up her father, makes dinner, does the laundry, and becomes the family counselor at age 13.

And, oh, how she hates her brother who seems unaffected by all this! He comes and goes as he wishes. He feels no compulsion to stay and fix things. It's not his fault; he won't buy into it. He's got his own life to live. And, so, he incurs the righteous indignation of the poor little one caught in a trap that has made her old before her time.

Or maybe it's simpler than all that. Some people have a stronger sense of responsibility than others. They take burdens upon themselves willingly. The needs of others always weigh upon them. Most of the time, this way of life is fine. But there are days when resentment builds – they carry so much while others seem to skate along: How can it be that other people find God so easily while I struggle every day to be faithful and get nowhere? How can that person just waltz in here after the rest of us have held things together for so long?

I experience the elder brother's anger when I feel that everything depends on me, and no one appreciates my obvious contributions to the maintenance of the cosmos. I begin to squirm over my toil. No one is helping me. Why do I have to slave away at this when no one cares? When my children were younger, I used to serve my family this peevishness as I served breakfast. My attitude said, "Here's the food your loving father has made for you, you ungrateful wretches!" All the time I was blocking the joy in my life.

In such a state, I would fail to see how the love that I have for each of my children could flow through such simple tasks as pouring cereal. I would fail to notice *them*. Now that they are older and three have left the house, I see what joy I squandered in my hours of petty indignation.

Whether the task is as simple as making a meal or as serious as caring for an aged parent, those crushed by a sense of duty find that the work never ends. The temptation toward bitterness (and, so, to a disconnect with God) will be great. Elder brothers are prone to resentment. Their path to joy must be found beneath the surface level of circumstances.

You Are Always with Me

We said earlier that the father in the story is the source of a blessed life. His house is a celebration of abundance balanced with hard, but satisfying, work. Labor, for this father, is to live out one's full potential. There is joy in working his fields and contributing to his resources. In the midst of a famine, the father extends a generous hand and offers food. The father in the story represents God our heavenly Father. His house is our deepest home.

The elder brother was part of that vigorous house, but he lost his connection to the joy of its life. He could not find a reason for laboring to maintain it, and so it seemed to him a house of slavery.

The father replied to his peevish boy, "Son, you are always with me, and all that is mine is yours." The father assumed that the son desired to be with him. I wonder if the elder son had ever thought of that. This is a wonderful reversal. He didn't say, "I am always with you," implying something about himself, as if he hovered around the son, restricting his freedom; rather, "*You* are always with me."

What did the young man think of that? Perhaps he wanted to answer, "No, I'm not. I'm out working in the fields most of the time. The sun is there, making me thirst, sapping my strength. But you spend the day looking down the road for my brother. I don't see you until the end of the day, and we rarely have much to say."

> He already was with the father. All he had to do was become aware of that reality and enjoy it.

Then the father might clarify, "Look, you, my son, are right here, in my home, on our farm, doing our work. You are near me, you have access to me at all times. You can be with me whenever you want. I always have time for you, but I won't hound you while you are busy. I am always interested in what you are feeling and doing."

The joy he desired he already possessed! Already, he *always* was with the father. All he had to do was become aware of that reality and enjoy it. Jesus in this story is telling those of us who are elder brothers, frustrated and striving, that we already are with God. That is our status. God is not hovering over us to scowl when every duty is not perfectly completed. In all that we do, we already are with God. We may enjoy the house of blessing in which we already live.

What would it mean to you if God were to say, "Daughter, Son, you are always with me. It doesn't make any difference whether you are thinking of me; I am always thinking of you. I am keeping you with me." Every moment, we are with God. God is with us. We already are connected!

'All That Is Mine Is Yours'

The father also said, "And all that is mine is yours." I like to imagine the conversation that could have occurred when the elder son began thinking about this:

Son: "You mean I'm free? I could go off and spend all your money, and have parties and live away from home?"
Father: "Of course. That has always been an option."
Son: "I could ask for anything I want and get it?"
Father: "Yes."
Son: "I could quit, and the farm wouldn't fall into ruin?"
Father: "Of course not. It doesn't depend on you. You may contribute if you like and share in our harvest. But I have plenty of resources. You may go if you like. Do you want to leave your work and home now, like your brother?"
Son: "Yes. Well, no. Actually, I like being responsible; I really have always

liked being at home. I just get tired sometimes of all I have to do."

Father: "Leave the burden of the harvest to me. I'll see to that."

Son: "But don't you want me to do better? Aren't you going to tell me to earn my way?"

Father: "Son, you are already with me. You already have all that I have. Now, come into the party. It's all right to celebrate. The work will keep. Your brother has just returned to his senses and come home. He was dead and is alive again. He is back with us. He was lost and is found."

There is a lifting of a burden in the father's words. No more striving is needed. Right now, already, all that God has is ours. God is always with us. Our work, then, is the joy contributing to God's work: creating the estate of blessing that he offers to the world. And though we labor, the harvest does not depend on us. God is the master of the house. Our joy is to be living as those who already belong and already share in the life of God. We can leave if we want to; God's land will still be plowed; the harvest will still be reaped. We can take off if we desire, but we already know that, deep down, we don't want to go – particularly now that we know God is responsible. We need not sweat to prove our worth any more; we need not strive to get the inheritance. That is all done. It is all taken care of already.

> *Our joy is to be living as those who already belong and already share in the life of God.*

How can all this be true?

Because of the person and work of Jesus Christ. We will explore how Jesus has accomplished such a blessing for us throughout the rest of this book, and especially in Chapter Ten. We'll also be considering how Jesus leads us into truly and deeply experiencing this amazing reality of the Father's love and presence. For now, I invite you simply to try on these incredible declarations. Walk through the next week thinking and acting as if it were so: You already are with God your Father. All that he has is yours.

Moving Ahead

When we feel distant from God, it may be that we have taken the foreign road into the far country. Or it may be that we have stayed home and viewed our lives as duty without joy. Either way, Jesus' parable tells us that God stands ready to welcome us home. We are watched for down the road by the loving Father. We are implored to come in and join the party. It is time to start down the road to home, to come in from the fields of duty to the party, and to meet one another over the love of the Father. On the way, we learn that we have something to teach each other: some of us about going away, others about staying home. Together, we can learn what life is like laboring in the house of blessing.

Such an invitation has great appeal to me. Unfortunately, I realize that our spiritual lives unfold with a bit more complexity. After the initial joy of starting home, we will have some work to do. The old layers still need to be peeled away. The joy of discovering that we are with God and all God has is ours will fade soon if we do not continue to deal with the underlying issues.

In the next chapter, we will see how Jesus works through a woman's past to connect with the living water of God's presence in her life.

Questions for Reflection or Discussion

Read aloud the story of the elder brother found in Luke 15:25-32.

+ Make a list of the personality characteristics of the older brother. What does he live for?
+ When do you experience in your life as a constant responsibility?
+ What makes us resistant to the possibility that joy is so close at hand?
+ What reasons do you give for not going into the party?
+ Do you think the elder brother went into the party after the talk with his father? What would have prevented him? What might have inspired him?
+ What would it mean to hear in the depths of yourself God saying, "Son, daughter, you are always with me, and all that is mine is yours?"

Exercises

Work individually on one or more of the exercises below, then share them in the group. Afterward, consider doing the second exercise together.

+ Imagine that the elder brother decides to go into the party. After a while, he and the younger brother sit down together in a corner to discuss their father and the return of the younger son.

- If you are working alone, write a dialogue between the two brothers that explores the new situation of one brother's return home and another brother's presence at the party. Explore what will be needed for reconciliation between the brothers and between each of them and their father. You may want to bring the father into the conversation at some point.

- If you are working in a group, play out the conversation in pairs, with one partner as the older brother and the other as the younger. For a twist, invite a third person to be the father. At first, he will sit silently, listening. Then, after a few minutes, he could enter the conversation.

- Or work the conversations in teams, one as the older brother, one as the younger. Both could list their needs, their feelings, their interest in the new life with the father. Then talk back and forth as a team.

- Imagine that it is the next day. The older brother has been thinking about the conversation with his father and now wishes to take advantage of his newfound access. What does he say when he goes in to see his father? Write this conversation.

- One way to enter these stories more fully is to use poems or prayers written by others. Their very newness to us may be a helpful way to experience the stories on a different level. Read this line from St. John of the Cross:

My spirit has become dry because it forgets to feed on you.[1]

with these lines from a Gaelic prayer,

I am serene because I know thou lovest me.
Because thou lovest me, nought can move me from my peace.
Because thou lovest me, I am as one to whom all good has come.[2]

1   Appleton, George, ed.; *The Oxford Book of Prayer* (New York:, Oxford University Press; 1985) p. 139.
1   Ibid.

Chapter 4

EVERYTHING I EVER DID

If it were as simple as taking the first steps, then reconnecting with God would not be such a problem for us. We have so many images for the beginning of the journey: going home, getting sober, being born again, going into the party, turning a new leaf. But once our yearning awakens us, and we get going, the underlying issues of our separation from God also arise. They demand our attention. God calls us to go deeper toward a resolution of anything that disconnects us. And that can produce a new resistance in us.

"Without knowledge of self there is no knowledge of God. ... Without knowledge of God there is no knowledge of self."[1] So begins John Calvin's famous *Institutes*. There seems to be some interrelation between a growing awareness of God and an increased consciousness of our lives. One leads to the other; the absence of one prevents the other. We cannot plumb the mystery of our being without a knowledge of God. Just as surely, we get no further in reconnecting with God if we are not willing to be led to a more honest exploration of what makes us who we are. Jesus was an expert at taking people deeper into themselves. He brought to light the hidden places, and invited people to open themselves to his Father.

Once, in the region of Samaria, Jesus met a woman by a well at noontime. Their conversation was a steady spiral into the depths of the woman's life and a new understanding of God. In this story, we learn quite a bit about the way Jesus dealt with people. Overhearing this conversation, we even may hear him addressing us.

The Dailiness of Life

Jews considered the Samaritans to be traitorous, unclean half-breeds. Years before, the Jews in that region had intermarried with the Babylonian conquerors,

---

1 Calvin, John; *Institutes of the Christian Religion* (Philadelphia; Westminster Press; 1960) p. 1.1.1.

rejected portions of the Hebrew Scriptures, worshipped not in Jerusalem but on Mt. Gerazim, and failed to support a Jewish uprising against the Romans. So, the Jews of Samaria had become Samaritans. No one is so hated as those most like us in all but a few crucial ways. The Jews considered the Samaritans unclean; contact with them was disdained.

Jesus had a habit of entering territory not assigned to him by traditional roles.

Jesus passed through Samaria on his way north, and stopped by a well to rest. He saw a woman who had come to draw water. There was no one else around. The hour was noon, and no doubt it was hot in the blazing Middle Eastern sun. It was strange that she had come alone, to a well outside of town, at the hottest time of day. Usually, the women came in the morning or evening, and they came together for safety and companionship. There was some reason why this particular woman did not want the company of others.

She had come to perform the daily necessity of gathering fresh water. Each new day meant the long walk out with the heavy earthen jar, then the drawing from the well, and the trip back home with the full container weighing her down. Fetching water typified the drudgery of the daily routine. It was arduous, but unavoidable. At the time of this story, the Samaritan woman's labor was made harder by whatever reasons she had for coming alone at such an off-hour.

We, too, know what it is like to be caught in the dailiness of life, and how our routine may be shaped by our own particular pain. There are the repetitive tasks, the constant requirements that can make one day blur into another so that, at the end of a year, we hardly may remember where all the time went. What's more, the pain in our lives may be keeping us out of joint so habitually that we even may forget that it is not normal to draw water in the heat of the day. We may have lived without

We know what it is to be caught in the dailiness of life.

kind words for so long that we no longer expect them. The ache of a betrayal may have been with us until hollowness seems like a natural feeling. We may have borne the pain of separation in relationships for enough years that we have grown to rely upon it as part of our daily rhythm.

An Interruption in the Routine

And then, one day, the Samaritan woman's routine was broken by the presence of a man at the well. Her guard went up – she knew about men. He asked for a drink. She sized him up and replied, "How is it that you, a Jew, ask for a drink from me, a woman of Samaria?" Jesus had broken the agreed bounds of conversation. Rabbis did not speak to women in public. Contemporary Jews avoided dealings with Samaritans; certainly, sharing a drinking vessel would have made one feel filthy.

Jesus had a habit of entering territory not assigned to him by traditional roles. We may well have feelings similar to the woman's. How can it be, Jesus, that you want something of me? I am not one of your saints. Churchy people may hang on your every word, but not me. It's doubtful that you will find in me something religious that you might need. I thought we agreed long ago that I wouldn't bother you if you wouldn't bother me.

Jesus countered by turning the discussion around. "If you knew the gift of God and who it is that is saying to you, 'Give me a drink,' you would have asked him, and he would have given you living water." The conversation switched from what she had to offer to the gift of God. Jesus tantalized her with the implication that what he had to give was highly desirable.

For us, to enter such a conversation with Jesus would open an opportunity we yearn for, if only we could realize it. Here is the possibility that there is a gift of God we may receive. God waits to give us something wonderful and important. We may feel that Jesus need not look to us for something religious, since we are not that type. But he answers that, long before we get spiritual, he has a gift for us - so attractive that, if we knew he had it, we would be aching for it.

But the Samaritan woman was not so easily taken in. Perhaps this was another line from yet another man. She looked him over again.

"Sir, you have nothing to draw water with, and the well is deep. Where do you get that living water? Are you greater than our father Jacob? He gave us the well. ..." This stranger who broke social customs out in the hot sun had no visible means to give her any gift at all. How could he change her life of routine? Did he have some secret?

We very well might ask Jesus ourselves, "Really now, what do you have to give me? Can you possibly have something that has anything to do with my daily life? You have no bucket and the well is deep. You are not relevant to the complexities of the relationships I am in. I've always thought that God wants it done by the book, everything neat and clean. I am far away from that. You do not know about the pressures of my business. You want things straight, but 10 people pull me from every direction. Surely, you are just gentle Jesus from Sunday school, the man with the golden rule, a god of sweet morality that never existed. What do you know of my life in the hot sun making noon runs for water out of fear of being seen by others?"

"Jesus, are you greater than the way of life I have inherited? Are you more than what the church and my parents have told me of you? Are you greater than the urges in me to live life the way I do and seem unable to stop? Honestly, I don't see anything in you that looks like it could be a gift to me. You are just old Jesus, odd and religious with little to say about practical life. I doubt you can pull this off."

An Offer of the Source

Jesus countered with a description of just what his gift could do for the woman. He gave her a knowledge of God, which would lead to a knowledge of herself. "Everyone who drinks of this water will be thirsty again, but whoever drinks of the water that I will give him will never be thirsty forever. The water that I will give him will become in him a spring of water welling up to eternal life."

He offered the possibility of never being thirsty at noon in the desert sun again. The dailiness of life revolves around perpetual thirst, and we return to the well again and again without any final satisfaction. Jesus offered an inner source that constantly could quench a person's thirst with fresh waters. A symbol of routine, the drawing of water, could become through Jesus' gift an image of refreshment. Receiving the gift of God through Jesus would renew her life.

There is a source that can transform daily life from drudgery and stale water to the gush of living water. Jesus offers living water as a spring that is within us. Its waters well up inside us, gush through us, and give meaning to all of life. The very ordinariness of our days can be enlivened with this splashing, clear, cool water.

> *Living water means continual renewal ... washing us in joy.*

Living water brings refreshment. It means continual renewal. Cleansing water flows through, washing us in joy. In living water, we have the hope that we do not always need to be cynical and cranky, to be dry and tired. Rather, love and thankfulness can well up through us. This is the possibility of living from the source, of being connected to the wellspring of our lives. The writer of the 87th Psalm knew that God is the source of living water when he prayed, "All my springs are in you."

What We Give in Exchange

The woman wanted this gift, if only to save her the daily trip to the well. "Sir, give me this water, so that I will not be thirsty or have to come here to draw water." Sure, if he could give it to her, she wanted it. It seemed like a nice convenience. Why not have a constant source of water, particularly if it was free? The woman's response considered living water on a literal level. It was a way to make life easier without any work on her part.

Similarly, at first we may begin work on a relationship with God because we hope it will solve our problems and make us happier. We hope that God will let us live pretty much as we do, with the new twist that we finally enjoy it. I'd like a relationship with God if it means I won't have any dull days, lonely nights, conflicts at work or financial worries. Yes, since it's free, wave the magic wand – give me the living water.

Of course, it doesn't work that way. We don't tap the spring of living water without descending into the depths of our being for a truth-telling session with God. He has designed us with a kind of spiritual "fail-safe" mechanism. We don't connect to the power and reality of God unless we are serious about knowing him and being known by him. We only receive God in proportion to our openness about ourselves before God. So, the casual dabbler in a conversation with Jesus will leave disappointed. The knowledge of God that is living water will require a commensurate, deepening knowledge of self before him. Jesus is not afraid to lead us to such an encounter.

He did not hesitate to urge the Samaritan woman deeper. "Go, call your husband, and come here." Jesus replied as if saying, "So, you do want what I have. Well then, let's talk, let's deal with your life. I know who you are. Go get your husband."

She answered him, "I have no husband." She wanted to talk about something else. The Samaritan woman tried to seal off that subject with her terse reply. We may feel, as well, that there are some areas we would rather not have Jesus bring up. We will try to close him off. Our replies might sound like these:

+ Look, you can be Jesus and we can talk religion, but don't meddle with closed subjects. There's no need to probe around about the broken relationships I have been through. I got through it then, and I can get along just fine without interference now.
+ Listen, you have no right to bring up my parents' expectations and the years I spent trying to please them. I have no need to prove myself any more.

- Jesus, just drop it. The cheating that I did was years ago. It's a dead subject. I have forgotten it, why don't you leave it alone? I have no more guilt. Really.
- What? Yes, of course I like my work. Every job requires sacrifice; every company puts on pressure. How I handle it is not your concern. I have no conflicts with work.

Life doesn't always turn out the way we had hoped. We make the best we can of it; we do the daily routine. And we deny there is a problem. Secretly, we want more, but we do not like for God, or others, to ask about these private yearnings. We try to deflect such probings.

Telling Us Who We Are

Jesus, though, was not put off by the woman. "You are right in saying 'I have no husband,' for you have had five husbands and the one you now have is not your husband. What you have said is true." Jesus became relentless. He named her life. He said, in effect: "I know you. I know who you are. There is no need to hide." How he knew, either by divine intuition or by her reputation, is not the point. Exactly what she had done or not done to live through five husbands is not the point. The issue was that she was a woman in guilt and denial who lived by avoiding the other women. He had a gift for her but, to receive it, she would need to own up to her life.

Similarly, Jesus might reply to the denials used above:

- "You are right in saying you can get along without my interference; you will merely continue to receive the loneliness you choose."
- "You are right in saying you have nothing to prove; you simply will feel unworthy all the time."
- "You are right in saying you have no guilt; it has turned to a constant numbness."
- "You are right in saying you have no conflicts at work; you gave over your soul and you are sinking."

Overcoming Resistance

No one likes to admit such brokenness. So, the woman used a tactic that always has been popular. She threw up an unanswerable religious question. Her reply tossed it all back on Jesus. "Sir, I perceive you are a prophet. Our fathers worshipped on this mountain but you [Jews] say that in Jerusalem is the place where people ought to worship." She brought up the old conflict between Samaritans and Jews about holy places. Jesus had gotten awfully close to breaking down the traditional barriers, so she threw one back up.

When Jesus gets too close to naming us and making us deal with the complexities of our lives, we, too, may tote out the religious arguments. We sense that God is making a claim on us. Jesus wants to dredge up the truth we keep well hidden. So, we may reply: "Well, what about the Buddhists? Will they be saved if they are good people? What about the problem of suffering in the world? How could an all-

> *There are no more questions except, 'What will you do with me?'*

powerful, all-loving God allow that pain? Isn't religion up to the individual?" We use these standard doubts, which are perfectly legitimate (but unanswerable) questions to keep God at bay. Since these contradictions will not be solved any time soon, they make excellent defenses against interacting with Jesus about the state of our own lives.

Of course, we cannot minimize the pain within such questions, nor the suffering that leads people to voice them. That very pain, though, can lead us down to the depths beneath the cover-ups. The woman's suffering in part was the Samaritan sense of inferiority, combined with her own sense of being ostracized.

Jesus, in his relentless love, took her still deeper: "Woman, believe me, the hour is coming when neither on this mountain nor in Jerusalem will you worship the Father … God is spirit, and those who worship him must worship in spirit and truth." He went beneath the questions of where and how to the question of *truth*. The knowledge of God and the knowledge of self remained intertwined. Spirit and truth require an inner honesty. God desires worship from the heart.

She made one final play at getting away. "I know that the Messiah is coming. … When he comes, he will tell us all things." This should have been a show stopper. The Messiah was always coming, but never came. This was like saying, "One day I will get to that, when things slow down," or, "One day we will understand, but for now all is a mystery." One day is safely in the distant future.

In reply, Jesus simply took off the gloves: "I who speak to you am he." He pinned her, communicating that, "There is no escape. The time is now. I am come to reveal your life to you and to reveal God to you. I have living water. There are no more questions except, 'What will you do with *me*?'"

At this point, they were interrupted by the return of the disciples. The woman, though, left her water jar and ran back to the town. She said to everyone, "Come, see a man who told me all that I ever did! Can this be the Christ?"

As the story concludes, we do not see any great work of healing, or hear of any particular response made by the woman. Somehow, though, being known was enough to ignite her life. The woman who drew water in the noonday heat in order to avoid people now ran to tell everyone what had happened.

To Be Known

There is something marvelous about being known. Many of us love to take personality tests and hear about who we are. When someone describes us, in love, for all our quirks and uniqueness, we may laugh with involuntary delight. We long to be discovered. While we may hide much from others, we nevertheless ache to have them find our hiding places.

The Father desires that we feel known by him, known fully and still loved. Such intimacy, though, requires our participation. By acknowledging what God reveals to us about ourselves, we can cooperate with the Spirit who searches out our depths. This confession in itself is healing. Vivid energy is released as suppressed aspects of ourselves are brought to the light of day and offered to Jesus.

Anglican priest Christopher Bryant wrote of this in his book *Jung and the Christian Way:*

> Directly I change my attitude and admit my fault or my folly, not merely verbally but with a real inward alteration of feeling expressed in outward behavior, then at once the healing waters begin to flow as from some deep spring within myself; the parched desert begins to blossom, and I am inundated with a sense of peace ... the renewing grace of God begins to heal and liberate those who turn and submit to this inner law. ... The life renewing Spirit flows from the belly, the symbol of a centre within us which is also the seat of powerful emotion. The belief that God guides us from the centre of our being can completely transform the idea of obedience to God's will.[1]

1   Bryant, Christopher; *Jung and the Christian Way* (London; Darton, Longman and Todd; 1983) pp. 43-44.

2   Calvin; *Institutes*; op. cit.; p. 1.1.1.

I remember going on a retreat once with two friends from the church. As the weekend progressed, our discussion grew more intimate. I decided to reveal a side of myself of which I have never been pleased, which I keep as well hidden as possible. I said, "I know that I try to be a nice, caring guy toward you most of the time, but if our friendship continues to deepen, you need to know this about me. I really can be a self-centered, attention-craving, egotistical person." I said it in all earnestness, with no small degree of fear. My friends started to laugh. I asked what was so funny. They howled. "Do you think you're telling us anything new? We know who you are. We love you just the same." What I feared to confess for fear of rejection was a fact completely obvious to my friends. They knew and they still cared. Once I admitted it, though, the release was like living waters refreshing me.

Jesus offered the woman at the well a spring of living water within her. He offers it to us, as well. The price is allowing him to take us into our pasts, into our brokenness, into the sins that we have done and the sins that have been done to us. We discover there that he knows us completely. And he asks that we allow him into those deep places to love us in great, forgiving intimacy. Calvin knew the healing side of such exploration:

> Accordingly, the knowledge of ourselves not only arouses us to seek God, but also, as it were, leads us by the hand to find him.[1]

Questions For Reflection

The story of the Samaritan woman is found in John 4:1-42.

+ In what ways have you felt about Jesus as the woman initially did: "Sir you have nothing to draw with and the well is deep?"
+ What does "living water" mean to you?
+ Complete the sentence, "If living water were welling up within me, I …."
+ In what areas are you most likely to try and deflect Jesus' inquiries?
+ In what areas of your life would you most like to be known, to be found out and still loved?
+ Imagine that Jesus does know all of you, and names those places long hidden. How would you respond?

Exercises

Work through the exercises below and discuss in your group as people feel comfortable.

+ Learn the line from the story, "Sir, give me this water, so that I will not be thirsty." When you have learned it well enough to say aloud without referring to your book, take a walk in which you repeat the phrase. Say it with different emphases, in different moods. Try singing it. You can begin simply by lengthening the sounds of the words. Try different tunes as they come to you; do not worry about being musical. Concentrate on expressing the emotion of the phrase.
+ Draw a picture of living water welling up within a person, perhaps yourself. Use the vivid colors of crayons, bright markers or water colors. A literal rendering is not the goal but, rather, an expression of the feeling of living water gushing forth.
+ Reflect upon your drawing. Thinking in terms of yourself, where does the living water get blocked? Where does it flow freely? Where is God, or the source, located?
+ Prayers from other traditions can provide new entrances to Bible stories. Try on this prayer from the Russian Orthodox tradition:

> O Savior fill my thirsting soul with the waters of godliness,
> as Thou didst cry to all: If anyone thirst, let him come to me
> and drink! O Christ God, Fountain of our life, glory to Thee!

> The Samaritan Woman came to the well in faith: she saw
> Thee, the Water of Wisdom, and drank abundantly! She
> inherited the Kingdom on high and is ever glorified.[1]

---

1   *The Divine Liturgy* (South Canaan, Pa.; St. Tikhon's Seminary Press; 1977) pp. 192, 194.

Chapter 5

Do You Really Want Something From *Me?*

Luke 5: 1-11

In the last three chapters, we have considered stories in which God is *offering* something to people like us. First, in the story of the two sons, Jesus told us through the younger brother that God our Father offers to receive us home when we have been far away. Second, the story of the older brother reveals that all the joy that the Father has is ours if we would simply go into the party. And, third, Jesus offered the woman by the well an unending supply of fresh, energizing, living water. He offers the gift of knowing us as we truly are, beneath the surface, and loving us even in these hidden places.

God wants us to reconnect with him. In each of these three stories, God promises to satisfy a particular deep yearning within us: for forgiveness, for joy and for intimacy. The possibility that even a portion of what Jesus described could be ours is enough to get us moving back toward God. We want to seek one who can give us so much.

But how do we find him? How do we get connected? Are there conditions? Is there a particular path we must follow to get home to God? Yes, God does indeed set some terms for how we are to meet him. In these next three chapters, we will look more closely at the other side of these gracious offers. We will consider what Jesus wanted from the people he encountered. We will weigh what it cost for them to open up their lives to his way of doing things. And each time we will ask how we might be able to stand up to such demands.

Put Out Into The Deep

One morning, during the first days of Jesus' ministry, he was teaching by the Sea of Galilee. As the listening crowd grew, people began to press in upon Jesus. Jesus needed a better vantage point for speaking. He saw two boats tied near shore and recognized one of the owners, named Simon, whom Jesus later would rename as Peter. Simon was busy cleaning his fishing nets. Jesus got into a boat and asked Simon to ease it out a bit onto the lake. There, the crowds could see him and Jesus could breathe.

When he was finished, he said to Simon, "Put out into the deep, and let down your nets for a catch." Simon answered, "Master, we toiled all night and took nothing. But at your word I will let down the nets."

So, these fishermen went against their professional instincts. They made for deep water and threw in their nets. Suddenly, they caught so many fish that the nets began to break. Simon called for his partners in the other boat. But even with two boats, the weight of all those fish began to sink the vessels.

Can a fisherman ever have too many fish? It was the kind of catch Simon might have dreamed about years ago when, as a sleepy boy, he tried to stay awake during the long nights while his father taught him the trade. But in this moment, Simon didn't care a thing for the fish. The boat was sinking and, with it, his means of a livelihood. Yet, even that wasn't his main worry. Simon fell down before Jesus. Water and fish swirled around him. He said: "Depart from me, for I am a sinful man, O Lord."

The miracle of the great catch opened up for Simon a sense of wonder. In a profound way, he realized the power and immediate presence of God. But this wondrous sight was followed by a striking awareness of unworthiness. Simon had a sudden gasp of realization, "If this is the Lord before me, I am not worthy, and I am in a lot of trouble!" The miracle became a horror. Just as God drew near, crashing in on an ordinary moment, Simon acutely felt his own sinfulness. He cried out to get some distance between himself and this holy presence.

> He realized the power and immediate presence of God.

Let's return to John Calvin for a moment:

> Again it is certain that man never achieves a clear knowledge
> of himself unless he has first looked upon God's face, and then
> descends from contemplating him to scrutinize himself.[1]

If our reference point is other people, we may have a fairly rosy view of ourselves. We prop each other up in the delusion that we're generally OK because

---

1   Calvin; *Institutes*; op. cit.; p. 1.1.2.

we fall within the range of what normal people are like. In fact, we may never even think about such things as "righteousness" or "sinfulness." These are words we seldom use in contemporary culture. Our ideas of living a good life come from looking around us at others, rather than "upward" toward any transcendent standard. As long as this remains the status quo, Calvin tells us, we live in a fog about who we really are. But should the reality of God invade our normal lives, we suddenly realize that there has been a much higher expectation upon us than we ever admitted. In the face of such brilliance, we feel hopelessly dull. Before such power, we feel pathetically weak. Before such *thick* reality, we feel thin and hardly alive. To use more spiritual terms, before such holiness, we feel acutely the reality of our sin and separation from God.

> *In the face of God's brilliance, we feel hopelessly dull.*

No wonder people avoid God! His light ferrets out all our dark places. Of course, we instinctively want to avoid such uncomfortable exposure.

That morning, Simon probably figured he was doing all right. Though the night's fishing had been frustrating, Simon still had steady work, good companions and a family at home. Looking at himself by comparison to others, most days he probably thought he was a good guy. But when he suddenly contemplated himself in the presence of an almighty power, his estimation changed. In the moment he should have been rejoicing at his good fortune, he was on his face begging Jesus to leave him.

We have seen that God offers us forgiveness, joy and intimacy. But in doing so, he demands a relentless honesty from us. He calls us out from delusion. He jerks our attention up from limp comparisons with our peers to see that God is the one with whom we have to deal.

What does he want from us?

He expects the courage to see ourselves as we really are from the perspective of the one who designed us. The younger son had to come awake to himself and see the disgrace to which his self-centered choices had led. The older brother had to have his jealousy, envy and legalism exposed if he were to come into the party. The woman at the well had to face the brokenness in her relationships as she encountered the one who could give her the healing waters of new life. Simon had to fall on his face desiring nothing but relief from the relentless pressure of God's holy presence before he could be ready to receive the calling Jesus had for him.

This is no fun. We hate to admit the reality that there is such a thing as sin

51

committed in thought and deed before a righteous God. That seems like talk better left for ignorant fundamentalists and sweaty television preachers. But here is the relentless truth. There is no reconnecting with God our Father, who loves us, without realizing and admitting our sinfulness. Not just our brokenness,

> *There is no reconnecting with God without admitting our sinfulness.*

our weariness, or our loneliness, but also our *wrongness*. We have to be willing to put out into the deep waters. There, beyond the comfortable shores of our daily routine, God brings the truth to us. Out of the depths comes the reality of our plight. We are helpless before God. We have not lived even according to what light we had. No excuses will help us. We are not victims. We are perpetrators. We are desperately wicked. And in dire need of mercy, we cannot earn, steal, or scam.

When we are honest enough to own up to this, we are in just the position where God will meet us.

Do Not Be Afraid

Jesus neither confirmed nor denied Simon's admission that, "I am a sinful man." Simon, after all, was not telling Jesus something he didn't know! Rather, seeing Simon at the point of raw, honest need, Jesus spoke right through Simon's fear: "Do not be afraid; from now on you will be catching men." The effect of those words was to say, "I know who you are and I have something for you to do; do not fear what you are not; I will make you into something more." Jesus accepted his confession. Jesus acted as if he himself had

> *At Simon's point of raw, honest need, Jesus spoke right through his fear.*

the authority to forgive sins and, in fact, had already done so. His very presence was an absolution. The miracle had brought Simon to his knees; Jesus lifted him up with a word of assurance: *Do not be afraid.* Just that quickly, the moment of horror was ended. The past was swept away and a new future was opening.

Casting nets for fish was finished. Could Simon have fished again after this great haul anyway? His life's work had been filled up and overflowed so magnificently that any future pursuit of mere fish would have seemed trivial. Now, Jesus asked Simon to go fishing for *people*. He wanted help from Simon and the others. Their new task would be to drop nets in a broken world whose people needed to be hauled into Jesus' healing presence. It almost goes without saying that, when they brought their boats to shore, they left everything and followed Jesus.

Jesus brought Simon into an encounter with reality. He showed Simon his sinfulness and God's forgiveness. He also brought Simon beyond the boundaries of daily experience. Simon saw that there is much more to life than the struggle to make a living and the routine of work. Jesus had arrived to call back the world to the love of his Father. He invited the disciples into that love, but not just so they could bask there. Jesus wanted workers who would join him in his mission. God came to us in Christ to offer us everything our souls yearn for. He also came to enlist us in his work of reclaiming the rest of his lost children.

The Drama of Transformation

What happened to Simon followed a pattern of God's dealings with us. Indeed, we see that something similar had happened centuries earlier. In the sixth chapter of the book of Isaiah, we read how the prophet had a vision of the throne of God. As he realized what he saw, his wonder immediately became dismay. Isaiah cried out: "Woe is me! For I am lost; for I am a man of unclean lips, and I dwell in the midst of a people of unclean lips; for my eyes have seen the King, the LORD of hosts!" He saw the pure glory of God and felt how unclean he was. But just as in Simon's story, God immediately responded to a deep, honest confession with healing forgiveness. In the next moment, one of the heavenly creatures around the throne flew down to Isaiah and touched his lips with a fiery coal. He declared: "Behold this has touched your lips; your guilt is taken away, and your sin is atoned for."

Right after such a "Fear not," there came a call to a particular task. Isaiah heard the voice of the Lord saying, "Whom shall I send, and who will go for us?" Isaiah replied, "Here am I! Send me."

This process moved Isaiah, as it did Simon, through awe to unworthiness to acceptance of a mission. Each was taken out of fear by a declaration of forgiveness, followed by a request for service. Their response to such a dramatic calling was one of complete commitment.

The very same drama may be played out, though often in subtler ways, in our lives today. Many people have undergone a season of transformation at some stage in their lives. It may not be recognized until years later. But, upon reflection, the pattern is clear: There was a growing awareness of God's reality in conjunction with a personal crisis. When the storm passed, there occurred a renewed commitment and deeper connection to God. Perhaps we can line out this process in an example:

Suppose you have been "plying your trade upon the seas." You've been living your life, working out things the best you can. You haven't been particularly interested in religion. It was part of your life as a child, but hasn't meant much recently. God may seem the right thing for sweet innocents, but none of them would understand the things you have thought and done. The idea of active faith seems too legalistic, too concerned with petty righteousness. You can't imagine yourself being a Bible-toting, hymn-singing, evangelistic, holy person. That would never do. You'd just as soon leave God alone if he'll leave you alone.

As the years have passed, though, more questions eat at you. Maybe it's because work has not turned out to be all you hoped. Maybe it's because the good life has meant more stress than happiness. Maybe it's just because you don't sleep like you used to. For whatever reason, you find you resonate with Simon, who had gone fishing all night but caught nothing. You've dropped your nets, hauled them in over and over, and there's nothing to show for it but a cranky mood and a tired body.

But then, the next day, there seems to be a subtle suggestion in your mind. Why don't you go ahead and go to church a couple of times? At least the family will be pleased. Or, why don't you go ahead and see the counselor? Let some of those feelings out; it can't hurt. Why not just talk with your spouse about how you're feeling? With so much water under the bridge now, there's nothing to lose. These hints toward looking up beyond yourself seem all very benign in the beginning. A tiny growl of spiritual hunger nudges you just a little way.

At first, it works out fine. It feels good to be at church. Talking an hour a week with the counselor eases the stress. Talking more with your mate has made everything easier at home. This bit of spirituality seems a better way to live.

But then, one day, there's another suggestion inside your mind that's a little more outrageous. "Put out into the deep and let down your nets for a catch." Think about the life that you live and know so well from a different point of view. What if it wasn't just about what you want and need, but about what God wants from you? What if you unfolded your nets, just let them down and took a look at what you've been living for all these years? Could you be bold enough to ask what you've been longing for in all these pursuits? Just unravel your nets in the deep and see what happens.

Suddenly, there might be a great haul of fish in the nets. It may be in church, or in the counselor's office, or over dinner with your spouse, or lying awake on your bed. But, quite dramatically, it dawns upon you: "There's more to life than what I have been seeing. There *is* a God. And God makes a claim on my life."

Perhaps, at the very same moment, you get a clearer view of yourself. The scales fall off your eyes. It is horrible. "I've been living for me. I've been curved in on myself all these years and it makes me sick. All the love lost! All the betrayals by neglect as much as anything! The blindness! I'm a mess that can't be fixed. I've got to close all these thoughts up and get out of here." Your boat is sinking.

But then, if you are blessed, just as soon as the horror of self-knowledge is embraced, there comes another feeling of presence. A gentle voice that speaks from the depths of the soul, even from the depths of the universe: "It's all right. Do not be afraid. I know who you are. Forgiveness is mine to grant. I'm not here to destroy your life. I'm here to remake it." It feels like death at first, but then there is new life. The Isaiah passage echoes within you: "See, this coal upon your lips makes them clean. I remove your sins."

> "Do not be afraid. I know who you are. I'm here to remake your life."

The sudden apprehension of God's reality creates a new and devastatingly realistic knowledge of self. You perceive a horrible gap between yourself and God. Immediately into the admitted breach, though, God pours love and forgiveness. There is an intuition that your Father knows fully who you are and loves you anyway. Beneath the crisis of the meaning of life, whatever form it takes, God gives a sense that all is well and you are kept in love. Jesus lifts you out of the sinking boat.

But there always is one more act in the play. The sense of God's claim comes again, not to undo you with unworthiness, but to rouse you to a higher calling. "Whom shall I send?" the Lord asked. Isaiah responded with all his heart: "Here am I. Send me." Jesus said, "From now on you will be catching people." And when they got to shore, they left everything and followed him. In contemporary language, your response may be, "OK, I'm yours. I'll live as your child; I want what you want more than anything. I need your love that much. I will serve you."

The New Occupation

Such a commitment may occur gradually over time, or in a burst of devotion. Either way, from the time we become consciously aware of Jesus' calling, our ordinary life ceases more and more to occupy center stage. We live for something deeper and higher. The work we do, we know now, could be burst through with such a fulfillment that it would make us quake. All that we strive for, which we used to think was so important to our happiness, could be fulfilled in a moment and we would count it worth nothing in the face of our Father God's love and forgiveness.

The tugs and ambitions we feel pale in comparison to the call of Jesus to follow him and go fishing for people. We discover that life is about being transformed by Jesus' love, and then going to offer that love to others.

This new activity of fishing for people may or may not be externally different from our current daily work. The key change is in the perspective from which we view people and tasks. We live now with a new sense of purpose in life: We are to be channels of God's love. We have a mission.

This may seem frightening, if we barely have begun to realize how much God loves us. It may seem impossible that we should be calling other people to the love of God when we have just arrived home, just stepped into the party, just had a first sip of living water.

But there is a principle of flow in the life that is connected to God. Jesus never intended his healing love to sit stagnant inside us. Living water bubbles and gushes as it passes into us, through us and out of us.

I am aware that following this story all the way to its dramatic conclusion may have leapfrogged us beyond where you are at the present time. Such an encounter of finding God may be more than you have yet known. Such commitment as asked of Simon and Isaiah may be too much at this stage.

So, before we further consider our mission, we will look at several other approaches to the way Jesus claims us. We will listen more intently to what Jesus asked of people and watch more closely for the way he provided his love and purpose for our living.

Questions for Reflection

The story of the great catch of fish is found in Luke 5:1-11.

+ For what do you cast your nets daily? When have you felt like you've been out all night and caught nothing?
+ Using the imagery of the story, in what waters might God be calling you to let down your nets into the deep? That is to say, in what areas of your life do you feel God might be nudging you toward a greater openness for transformation?
+ How might God desire to reorient the work of your life?

- Simon was struck with a sense of his unworthiness in the face of the miracle. Are there ways in which you feel unworthy of God's love and attention? What reassurance would help you?
- Can you remember an experience of awe, the feeling of being in the presence of something or someone very much greater than yourself, an experience that also evoked a feeling of humility?
- Today, getting more than we could imagine of what we work for might simply make us feel inflated with pride. But how might God so overflow the strivings of daily life to open your eyes to the deeper purposes in living?
- How can we today be fishermen and women of people? How might such a vocation be worked out in your life?
- What would it mean to you to be able to do something for Jesus, to carry out a work for him?

Exercises

- Try on this poem by George Herbert as a prayer. In it, the poet imagines being invited by God to sit down for an intimate meal. He feels reluctant and unworthy of such hospitality. But God, the host, insists on serving him. Let this poem lead you through an encounter with God that moves from unworthiness to being claimed by his love:

Love (3)

Love bade me welcome: yet my soul drew back,
    Guilty of dust and sin.
But quick-eyed Love, observing me grow slack
    From my first entrance in,
Drew nearer to me, sweetly questioning,
    If I lacked anything.

A guest, I answered, worthy to be here:
    Love said, You shall be he.
I the unkind, ungrateful? Ah my dear,
    I cannot look on thee.
Love took my hand, and smiling did reply,
    Who made the eyes but I?

Truth Lord, but I have marred them: let my shame
    Go where it deserve.
And know you not, says Love, who bore the blame?
    My dear, then I will serve.
You must sit down, says Love, and taste my meat:
    So I did sit and eat.[1]

• Using colored markers, draw a picture of your nets overflowing with what you strive for in your life. When you have completed your drawing, consider if this abundance is enough to satisfy you. Consider if the God who overflows the nets could give an invitation so compelling that you would leave the catch on the shore. Repeating the words, "Follow me and I will make you fishers of people," lay aside your drawing and imagine going to follow Jesus.

---

1   Herbert, George; "Love (3)" in Dawson, Gerrit Scott; *Love Bade Me Welcome: Daily Readings with George Herbert; op. cit.;* p. 217.

Chapter 6

How Can I Do This?

Mark 10: 17-31

Unfortunately, few of us have an experience as dramatic as Simon's great catch of fish. We do not get spectacularly overwhelmed either with God's presence or our own sinfulness. We seldom see our lives changed immediately. Truthfully, a big part of us doesn't even want such radical intervention in our routines. The kind of stories we are considering may even put off those whose search for God is still tentative. This is a sad fact of our humanity: resistance to the call of God is inevitable. Even though we yearn for God, we still balk at the terms offered. Far too often we sit thirsty by the well or lonely outside the party. And it is the issue of resistance that our next story addresses.

Once, Jesus was setting out on a journey when a man ran up, fell on his knees before him and asked, "Good Teacher, what must I do to inherit eternal life?" Immediately, we realize that the man was urgent. We later learn that he was very wealthy. This makes his actions all the more remarkable. He put aside all pride in his position to show respect to this rabbi from the rural north named Jesus. He wanted to be sure that he would be with God always. But this was more than just trying to get an insurance policy about the next life. The phrase "to inherit eternal life" had implications for today as well.[1] The man wanted to be sure he was living life *now* in accord with God's will. He wanted to connect with God in a way that was vivid and life-giving from this moment into eternity. He was searching for the living water, for the Father's homecoming feast, and for the One so real that you would leave even the greatest catch of fish to rot in order to follow him.

---

1   Lane, William; *The Gospel of Mark* (Grand Rapids, Mich.; Eerdmans; 1974) pp. 363-370. Professor Lane's excellent commentary on Mark has provided the historical background for this chapter.

Immediately, though, Jesus slowed the man down. He deflected the man's opening flattery. "Why do you call me good? No one is good but God alone." Strict Jews reserved the title of "good" for God. But the Greek culture of the time might use such a phrase liberally for esteemed teachers. Using these words, the man showed high reverence for Jesus in a culturally sophisticated manner. Jesus, however, took the opportunity to turn the attention from himself to his Father. He wanted the man to think as a simple Jew, not with the spirituality that was in vogue.

Jesus first answered the man's question with a standard instruction in piety. The way to a life of blessing, as everyone knew, was through keeping the law. "You know the commandments: 'Do not murder, Do not commit adultery, Do not steal, Do not bear false witness, Do not defraud, Honor your father and mother.'" This is an interesting list. All but "Do not defraud" are taken from the Ten Commandments. And these are the easier, more obvious of the commandments for a decent person to keep.

Jesus' list is about avoiding wrong behavior, but it doesn't say much about how to satisfy the hunger in our souls.

This list is like answering the question, "What does it mean to be a Christian?" with the reply, "Oh, you know, read your Bible, go to church, do unto others and try to be a good person." Those things are all part of being a Christian, but they don't get down to the essence.

What an insightful teacher Jesus was! He threw out a stereotypical answer to reveal the level on which the man was seeking. If this wealthy man merely had been a superficial seeker, simply wanting a stamp of approval for the way he was living, Jesus' answer would have been enough. He could have gone away, left in his self-satisfied shallowness. But a person with a restless soul could not easily accept that list as adequate for eternal life.

The man replied: "Teacher, all these I have kept from my youth." The implication was that he was not satisfied with standard religious observance. The man had lived a good life; he had been a good guy, one who did the right thing, but he needed more. This man was not the younger brother type who went off and squandered his inheritance; he was more like the older brother who stayed home and did what was required of him. Yet, he felt a lack in his soul.

Today, he would be someone who often has been in the church, no stranger to the language of faith. We could meet him in the pews. For instance, this could be the man who works hard during the week, comes to church on Sunday, sits respectfully, and has the admiration of his peers. He ushers two months a year, serves on a finance committee, and generally contributes his share of time and money. Usually, everything is fine but, once in a while, comes the nagging doubt,

> *The nagging doubt, "Is this all there is? Shouldn't I be feeling more?"*

"Is this all there is? Am I doing the right thing? Shouldn't I be feeling more?" The question of meaning arises. He wants to know more about what he needs to do in order to live as one passionately related to God.

Or, this may be the woman who has helped out at church in all the required ways. She has taught Vacation Bible School. Every week, she has dressed the children and gotten them to church in the typical Sunday morning mad dash. A hundred covered dishes have been received from her hands. When the prayer chain called, she prayed. Once a year, the circle met at her house. All these things she has done since her youth. And, still, she feels there is something missing. What else should she do?

One Thing You Lack

When the man had implied his dissatisfaction with standard religious observance, Jesus evidently was moved. Mark records this wonderful line: "And Jesus, looking at him, loved him." Of course, Jesus loved everyone he met. But articulating his love in this moment meant that something in particular had touched Jesus. The man's honest searching evoked Christ's affection. This feeling of love suffused Jesus' words in the next moment.

He spoke to this man with the hope of meeting his need: "You lack one thing: go, sell all that you have, and give to the poor, and you will have treasure in heaven; and come, follow me." For the man who had everything, one thing was missing – giving away what he had. What he lacked was not doing something more or obtaining something else; he needed to clear out some of what he had. His stuff was in his way. So, Jesus asked him to orient his entire life radically toward others.

It is important to realize here that Jesus' advice, as wild as it sounds to our ears, was even more astonishing in the culture of first century Judaism. This episode preceded the development of the Christian belief that poverty is a virtue of spiritual vitality. Rather, people felt that riches were a sign of God's favor. Having a lot meant blessings had been given in reward for righteous living. Of course, giving a tithe had been part of that culture, as well as the understanding that one should be open-handed toward the poor. But giving up everything would have been like tossing God's blessings back at him, a sign of disrespect. The man would have been making himself like the unrighteous and the unblessed; all signs of spiritual achievement would have been relinquished.

Looking at him, Jesus loved him, then asked him in love to strip himself of all signs of God's favor. He was to start again. Emptying out, not achieving more, was the way to inherit eternal life. Selling it all in order to bless the poor would clear the way to connect with God through following Jesus.

> *Emptying out, not achieving more, was the way to inherit eternal life.*

The Way of a Child

It is no coincidence that this story immediately follows the story of the blessing of the children. Previously, people were bringing their small children to Jesus in order that he might touch them and give them a blessing. The disciples didn't like all this crowding, and tried to send the people away. But Jesus rebuked them. He said, "Truly, I say to you, whoever does not receive the kingdom of God like a child shall not enter it." Then, he took the children in his arms and blessed them.

Once again, this story predates our culture. Judaism had not passed through a cycle of the adoration of children and the elevation of their needs. No cultural esteem for the innocence of childhood had made Jesus' words sentimental or even particularly welcome. Children were loved, of course, but economically they were unimportant. They could not achieve or produce. Children only could receive what was given. So, evidently, the Kingdom of God – this life of connectedness to all God has for us – is a gift for those without sufficient claim to it. And, in fact, all assertions of worthiness become a hindrance. The kingdom comes by grace alone.

This episode with the rich man appears to be in contrast to the story of the older brother we considered in Chapter Three. In that parable, the father said, "Son, you are always with me, and all that I have is yours." In this story of the rich man, Jesus said, "Sell all that you have and give to the poor … and come, follow me." On the one hand, all things are ours. Whatever we have been seeking already is within reach. All that God has, which is everything, has been given to us in Christ Jesus. But, on the other hand, nothing is ours. We may demand no rewards. Which is true? Are we those who can joyfully lay claim to all of God? Or, are we those who must live in poverty for Jesus' sake?

The crux seems to be our sense of *possession*. Again, the image of children is helpful. The child may partake of all his or her parents have. Every blessing and provision, every privilege, may be bestowed before any merit can lay claim to earning such abundance. The child may enjoy the parents' resources, but the child does not have legal entitlement, may not buy or sell at will, and may not supplant the parents.

When we are stripped of claims of achievement and worthiness, then we are open to receiving all. If we think we have leverage on God to demand a blessing, then we are blocked from it. If we feel we have enough on our own to satisfy us, we will know want in our spirits. If we hold to what we have as our own, then our dear heavenly Father – to open our eyes to the truth and for the good of our souls – will ask for it to be handed over. He will demand that we shift our focus from what we have accumulated to how we may give it to those in need. This outward movement will clear out room in our souls for the eternal life, the living water and festive abundance, with which God will fill us.

> *If we feel we have enough on our own, we will know want.*

Costing Not Less Then Everything

The heart of this passage is that Jesus, who came to give us his life, does indeed ask us for something. He asks for ultimate allegiance. He wants God his Father to be at the center of our being. Control is released into the hands of God; will is surrendered. My way must give way to God. The great poet T. S. Eliot has written that such simple relinquishment at the heart of our life with God is a state "costing not less than everything."[1]

We have uncovered the great paradox of the Christian faith. God desires to give us everything. God demands that we give up everything for him. When we hold on to what we have in defiance of what God requires, we are disconnected and cut off from the way of true, eternal life. When we are stripped of all achievement, when the hand opens and lets control slip away, then – and only then – does God respond with the gift of all things. So often, we are blocked from a life of connection and joy, not because the Father will not give, but because we will not release.

Of course, no one wants to do this. It seems against all reason to let go of what we have in hopes of what an invisible God may give. The man in the story, who came with such high hopes, could not immediately accept Jesus' words. Mark

---

1   Eliot, T.S.; "Little Gidding;" *Four Quartets* (London; Faber and Faber; 1944) p. 48.

tells us: "Disheartened by the saying, he went away sorrowful, for he had great possessions." Precisely what he possessed blocked him. The man was sad. Was he grieved because he knew that the whole of his young life had been spent managing his position and wealth? Was he sad because he soon would be giving up all he had both inherited and worked for? Was he astonished that all these years he had focused on the wrong thing? We do not know if he later took Jesus' advice or not.

But we can sympathize with his difficulty. We may find that we are so enmeshed in our way of life that change seems nearly impossible. Though we are lonely for a connection to God, old loyalties keep a grip on us. We feel locked into the expectations of our current lifestyle. So many people would be disappointed if we radically changed our life focus. Furthermore, it goes against our grain to have to count our achievements in the world as gaining no purchase on God's favor. We strive to be worthy of love and, yet, Jesus tells us that such pretension to worthiness only blocks us from receiving the worth the Father will confer upon us. This undoes all our usual patterns. Moreover,

> We are blocked … not because the Father will not give, but because we will not release.

control of one's affairs, taking charge, being the captain of the ship, making our own way – all are prized by our culture. How could Jesus ask us to give these up? Surely, he is not being literal about this?

We cannot say exactly what he asks of each person. It very well may be a literal giving up of things we prize more than God. It could be particular possessions or fanatically following a sports team. It could be keeping up the appearance of our home or climbing after success at work. It could be a particular lifestyle or an addiction to following a financial market. It could be that he asks for none of these things. Following Jesus does not necessarily mean entering a lifestyle of material poverty, or even entertainment deprivation. What he asks for, however, will be that which is keeping us from eternal life. He will want whatever has kept our focus on ourselves and not others. He will call us to an out-turned life that flourishes in caring for the needs of others. He will urge us to release whatever we have been using as a substitute for the true God of the universe. He will not let us make ultimate anything but himself. He desires to save us from all these little gods who inevitably disappoint us.

The possibilities of what he may ask for are frightening. This is particularly true if we know little of Jesus and have little reason to trust that a relationship with his Father will fulfill us. Jesus seems willing to take the risk that we will turn away from his demands. With the rich young man, Jesus went right for the heart. He did it in love, but he was no less demanding in his compassion. He wants it all. He insists that we meet him as children. We are simply asked to receive what he gives us in love. We cease to insist that we have earned anything. We dismiss the stories we have composed of our worthiness before God. We gamble all on Jesus' willingness to take us in his arms and bless us as he did the children.

> *Jesus has the power to transform you.*

Jesus' striking teaching may tempt you to put down these pages and go away disappointed, just as the man in the story did. You had hoped, perhaps, for something less invasive, something more fulfilling along the lines of what you always have believed makes for the good life. This story of Jesus can feel intolerable. In fact, the disciples were amazed, too, asking, "Then who can be saved?" Jesus looked at them and said, "With man it is impossible, but not with God; for all things are possible with God."

No one is so enmeshed in their present pursuits that God cannot release them. No god to which we have sold our souls has authority over our Father in heaven. He has the power to transform us. He can help us let go of those possessions and habits, memories and lifestyles that seem to have such a grip on us.

If you are still interested, there is a way to the eternal life that the rich young man sought. We shall attempt to follow it in the next chapter. Meanwhile, I commend to you the further reflections below, and especially the use of the Methodist Covenant Prayer this week.

Questions for Reflection

The story of the rich young man is found in Mark 10: 17-31

+ In what ways have you tried to your live your life as a 'good' person in the conventional sense? How has that been satisfying? What, if anything, is lacking?
+ The rich man asked about eternal life. If you could ask Jesus one question pertinent to the living of your life or receiving the life to come, what would it be?
+ Jesus asked the rich man to sell all he had and give it to the poor. What kinds of possessions, responsibilities, habits or activities may be blocking your following Jesus?

+ What do you fear Jesus will ask of you? What do you hope he will ask of you? From what demands would you turn away sad?

Exercises

+ Consider if you think the man finally did accept Jesus' instructions and sold everything. Write a paragraph in the next couple of days that tells what you think he did; perhaps you could write one from each perspective.
+ Then, write a paragraph in which Jesus says to you, "One thing you lack. ..." Explore what he asks of you and how you respond.
+ For those who want to respond to the claim of Jesus on their lives, try on this prayer from the Methodist Service of Covenant Renewal. Pray it every day this week in hopes that God will use it to loosen your hold on anything that is keeping you from following Jesus:

> I am no longer my own, but thine.
> Put me to what thou wilt, rank me with whom thou wilt:
> Put me to doing: put me to suffering:
> Let me be employed for thee or laid aside for thee:
> Exalted for thee, or brought low for thee:
> Let me be full, let me be empty:
> Let me have all things: let me have nothing:
> I freely and heartily yield all things to thy pleasure and disposal.
> And now O glorious and blessed God, Father, Son and Holy Spirit,
> Thou art mine and I am thine. So be it.
> And the covenant which I have made on earth let it be ratified in heaven.[1]

---

1   From the *Methodist Covenant Service*; excerpted in *The Oxford Book of Prayer* (New York; Oxford University Press; 1985) p. 217.

Chapter 7

IN THROUGH THE BACK DOOR

Luke 7:36-50

I still remember the spring afternoon years ago that was the turning point in some personal counseling I was undertaking. The therapist and I had talked for many weeks about my life and relationships. Being a dutiful patient, I had admitted freely many instances of selfishness and betrayal of which I was neither proud nor, to be honest, particularly ashamed. There was, of course, something else we were trying to uncover.

As we moved closer to it, whatever *it* was, I remember feeling more and more like a little boy. I grew increasingly embarrassed. Today, I do not even recall what it was I had to declare. I only know it was some admission of bald need, of wilting selfishness, of some little thing I had done that had no gloss of charm or style to it. It had no grandiosity of "big sin." It was just there, a raw little nugget of my essential neediness.

When I finally spoke it into the open air, I thought, "Now that will do it. She will realize how petty and childish I am. She will know that I have no big problem; she will discontinue the therapy. I don't deserve to be here anyway."

But my counselor did not flinch. Her expression stayed exactly the same as it had been. She listened and accepted. Of course, she knew what I was revealing. I think she could tell that I was ready to be filleted by the knife of truth. But there was no accusation. She simply received it as another part of me. We went on, and I was free.

I danced out of the office and laughed all the way home. People in the staid streets of that town stared at me, but I didn't care. I was free. Someone had seen inside me, to the worst pettiness, and still accepted me. My healing had begun. I was learning how to love – because I had been loved in that specific way.

In the last chapter, we saw that Jesus asked for "not less than everything" from the man who had approached him. Such a demand seemed almost impossible to meet; and perhaps you felt your own resistance arise to giving away yourself. Jesus' head-on approach may raise our defiance. But approaching God from a position of strength did not get the rich man very far; you can't get in that way.

In another story, Jesus took a different tack; the one who came to him led with her need, not her strength. Her story was resolved not in a sad walking away, but in peace and forgiveness. This may be a way in for us, as well.

Drawn To Find Jesus

In the seventh chapter of Luke, we read of a woman who heard that Jesus was in town and went to find him. She had a reputation in her village of being a "sinner." Luke does not tell us exactly what she had done, but the label seems indelible. I wonder what in Jesus drew her to him. Word may have reached the common people that Jesus was not intimidated by the rich or the righteous. He did not mind being seen with misfits. Jesus dared to put his hands on the sick. The forgotten were noticed by him. He looked at them; he spoke to them; he touched them.

Perhaps we can imagine this woman's thoughts as she made her way through the streets. She may have tried to recall how long it had been since anyone had touched her with tenderness. How long had it been since anyone had looked at her without first seeing the label of her sin blazoned across her face? Everyone in that tiny town knew who she was; there was never an escape. She had no place to go. If only someone would come for her. It had been months since anyone had even spoken kindly.

> *When did I not have the weight of these memories?*

"Was there ever a time," she wondered, "when I did not have the weight of these memories around my neck? Did I ever walk lightly through these streets? I am reminded always, every time I see someone, of who I am: a sinner. Joseph is a carpenter; Ruth is a seamstress; Ben is a priest; and I am a sinner. To them, I do no good. I have no occupation. I do not breathe or have needs or wonder about the weather like other people. I am simply a sinner. Touch me and touch sin. Speak to me and your tongue is filthy. Look at me and see the discarded."

So, she went to find Jesus. He was going to dinner at the house of Simon, a Pharisee. Such events normally were open to acceptable visitors. She would risk going; she could not help it. "What could a Pharisee do to me now anyway? Let him scowl; he does that all the time as it is. If only Jesus would let me near him; if only he might once look at me and see me for something other than my label, see the me behind my shame. One look; one touch; one word; I would give anything."

She brought with her an alabaster flask filled with perfumed ointment. It was one of the costliest gifts one could give. The expensive flask itself had to be broken in order to use the salve. It was a one-time, perishable gift, solely for the immediate comfort of the recipient. She had come hoping to offer a gift of extravagant love.

Tears Became Love

The woman entered the house, passing the other guests, ignoring their whispers. She made her way to the table, and no one dared to stop her. At last, she found that she was standing behind Jesus. As was the custom of the day, he was reclining at the table. His legs were stretched out to the side of him. The woman had never seen Jesus before; she knew him as the only stranger, and by something else she could not name. He did not turn around. But she began to cry.

She wept for the weight of it all – for all the reasons she should not be there, for all that she regretted. Oh, the wretched ash heap of her life! And she cried that she could do nothing else but go there. As usual, her life was out of control. She was ever swept along by forces she didn't understand. And she wept all the more as she realized she was standing so close to Jesus. He had seen her now, and she was still there. He had not rejected her out of hand.

"I wish I could touch him; just the least part of him; just his feet." And she saw that her tears were falling onto his feet, which were stretched out as he leaned on his side at the table. Then all her care in the world was for those feet. Her whole life, all her feelings and pent-up love fell in tears upon his tired, dirty feet. She pulled the clasp and let down her hair, defying the immodesty of it. She wiped his feet with her hair.

> *Her whole life fell in tears upon his feet.*

"Could I but soothe you for a moment?" she thought. "Will you have this comfort I can give? Do not turn from me now. Find ease from your travels; I can make your feet feel better. Oh, take my love. It is all I have and it is yours." She kissed his feet and poured the perfume on them. She could see that its sweet smell did seem to soothe his tiredness. Her gentle touch tended Jesus with love and adoration.

The Scandal of Forgiveness

For a moment, Jesus found ease in her gift. He closed his eyes to receive this brief comfort from the weight of his ministry. He did not dismiss her; he did not tell her to stop. Jesus did not turn away, though she revealed an embarrassing vulnerability before him in public.

When Jesus opened his eyes, Simon the Pharisee was glowering at him. Simon was furious. His thoughts raced: "How could he accept the ministrations of a woman such as this, and in my house, and in front of half the town? She has made a spectacle and he doesn't care. Why, it's obscene! If he were really a prophet of God, he would know what kind of woman this is who is touching him – a sinner."

Jesus knew who she was, and he knew that Simon was full of gall. Jesus answered his thoughts: "Simon, I have something to say to you."

Simon accepted the challenge. "Say it, Teacher."

"A certain money lender had two debtors. One owed five hundred days' wages, and the other fifty. When they could not pay, he cancelled the debt of both. Now, which of them will love him more?"

Simon was insulted by such an obvious question, but he still bit the hook and answered: "The one, I suppose, for whom he cancelled the larger debt."

Jesus then said, with words so simple they must have burned Simon, "You have judged rightly. Do you see this woman? I entered your house; you gave me no water for my feet, but she has wet my feet with her tears and wiped them with her hair. You gave me no kiss, but from the time I came in she has not ceased to kiss my feet. You did not

> *Her sins, which are many, are forgiven – ... for she loved much.*

anoint my head with oil, but she has anointed my feet with ointment. Therefore I tell you, her sins, which are many, are forgiven – for she loved much. But he who is forgiven little, loves little."

The woman could hardly believe what she was hearing. As she watched, Jesus turned to her again and said right to her, "Your sins are forgiven." He told her she was free. She was herself once more – not her label, not her past, not her shame.

"I'm me again," she thought. "I'm clean. The master said so! I am not a sinner any more. I am a woman, who sins, yes, but who is forgiven. My life is not my sin any more; my life is my love, and he is everything to me!"

Then, after all the guests had gasped and murmured that Jesus should dare to pronounce forgiveness – a prerogative reserved for God alone – for one such as she, he spoke again. "Your faith has saved you; go in peace."

Uncovering the Wounds Which Lead Us to God

There is no magic formula for connecting with God. The story of this woman tells us that there is only a unique, personal, messy encounter. The possibility is that if we went to him, he would accept us, and this nudges our souls toward Jesus. Like the woman of the village, we might be drawn to him if we heard he was in town. This raises the pointed question for us: "If you came and stood behind Jesus, finding that your presence was silently accepted, over what would you weep?"

The wounds that lead us to find Jesus are many and varied. They are difficult to face. We have tried to live as if they were not there, but the presence of Jesus uncovers their existence. Tears surge in even the hardest of us.

Over what would you weep?

We might cry for all the ways we have not been loved in the past – too many expectations, too much shame, too little attention, too much figuring it out on our own. We do not feel worth very much and our tears are made of anger as much as sorrow.

Sometimes, we are stricken to think of what we have done in the name of love to get what we needed that had been withheld. Or, worse, the ways we paid back those who did not meet our needs.

To grasp that what has been done cannot be undone might cause tears to come spooling out of our eyes in despair. The dead cannot be called back for reconciliation now; the marriage is over; the children have moved away; and there is nothing we can do any more about it.

Some of us have given away too much of ourselves, given to another person the devotion meant only for God. And we have seen that lesser hands have not held our hearts kindly. No one could handle such a gift, and our souls have been squeezed by another's fallibility.

Some have poured love down the pit of another's addiction, and all our intuition said it was the right thing to do. But, in that black hole, all the rules are reversed. Suddenly, we discover that we did not help, but contributed to the addiction. Our sacrifice was in vain, and we cry out.

Some of us have seized control over others. We have forcibly wanted to mold people into our image. We have wanted to be God and attempted to crush those who would not take the bait of that idolatry. Every moment is managed by us; an iron hand precedes us. Control cannot be dropped. And we are so tired from it. And so ashamed of all we have forced upon others. To be in the presence of one we cannot control or manipulate, one who simply is and remains loving, might move us to weep over the unwholesome fruit of our labors.

71

Some will cry that they have tried for so long to please that they have become master manipulators. They have received attention and power, but cannot trust it, for they always angled after it. They feel they must forever keep on earning acceptance – to let down the guard would be to freefall over the abyss of rejection. In the presence of Jesus, there is no way to earn his love. To stand behind him is to plunge into that void. And we cry in fear.

> *His very presence pulls it all out of us.*

Once the armor of our daily facade is cracked, there are a thousand, thousand things within us over which to cry: cruelty and the withholding of love; helplessness and giving away too much; betrayals and desertions; being left; plotting in spite. Turning from the truth, we knew to pursue what we wanted. Feeling empty, tired, dirty, without hope.

As the woman in the story wept, Jesus said nothing to her for quite a while. This silence of his is even more terrifying than what Jesus asks of us. His very presence pulls it all out of us. We come undone.

Of course, in this process, Simon the Pharisee continually urges us to quit, to leave Jesus, to go back home and behave. He hisses that we should keep our place – don't dare bother God. We need not try to change, for people such as we never can change. Simon, however, does not have the final word, nor does our fear or even our pain. Jesus receives the tears and does not reject us. He speaks the word of forgiveness. He pronounces peace and sets us on the way to wholeness.

The Stages of Healing Acceptance

This story offers a paradigm for the transformation Jesus brings to us. The stages of this process are crucial. They involve a dynamic interplay between us and Jesus. I can identify at least six movements in the story that may be seen in our lives as well:

1) The first move is his. *Jesus comes to town.* God arrives in our midst in Jesus Christ. Somehow, in the midst of our daily living, we hear that one such as Jesus exists and can be encountered. There is news that gives us hope: We can find God through encountering Jesus. Because he has come to us. He can make life different. Coming to town, being find-able, receiving sinners, working change in people's lives – all are God's work in Jesus. He initiates the connection.

2) The next move is ours. His presence draws us, *but we must be willing to go to him.* Knowing that being in his presence will set our wounds oozing and our

tears flowing, we yet summon the courage to go. In that embarrassing pain, the critical step of faith is to turn our shame into an act of love. We give him our failures and our pasts as an offering. We release them to him. With Psalm 51, we discover, "The sacrifices of God are a broken spirit; a broken and contrite heart, O God, you will not despise." In this way, we love him.

3) Jesus, of course, helps us. This is the third stage, occurring concurrently with our confession. The more we reveal, the more we discover that we are not rejected. The more we are accepted, the more likely it is that we will be moved to love and devotion. *He is very faithful to meet us almost immediately with a sense of forgiveness* if we will be honest and open in his presence. He declares, "Your sins are forgiven."

4) The fourth stage involves *the inevitable backlash* to this emerging grace. A voice of doubt arises. Simon the Pharisee appears, in the guise of those people who work against us, or as a voice within our minds. He reasserts our unworthiness and tries to make our situation seem hopeless. Simon only can be answered by the love of Jesus. We do not have the resources alone to combat him. Simon always knows enough about us to name our weak spots and create doubt. Within us, there is no adequate answer for him.

5) The reply that silences the Pharisee comes from Jesus. *He reaffirms our acceptance.* This is based not on our worthiness, but only on Christ's enduring love. The Pharisees always will have something on us. We can answer the accusation not by justifying ourselves, but only by naming the love that Jesus has for us. We might need to cling to this story as our only objective proof. Jesus answered Simon on behalf of the woman: "Her sins, which are many, are forgiven – for she loved much." Jesus is the one who then turns to us, as he turned to the woman, and says that, even amidst the accusers from our past, "Your faith has saved you; go in peace."

6) In response, the final movement in this first dance of transformation belongs to us. *We accept the word of forgiveness* and go our way, no longer bound to the habits, the labels and the destructive behavior that previously undid us. We are those to whom a word of Jesus has been spoken. We live for him.

There is a similarity between this story and the one about Simon the disciple and the great catch of fish. Both characters moved through apprehending the power of God in Jesus, to confessing their sin, to receiving forgiveness, to living a changed life with a new calling. The active love of Jesus made the difference in turning despair into joy. By contrast, the rich man in the previous story did not move into any position of confession or weakness. We did not see him coming undone within the timeframe of the account. He did not, at least immediately, give up his power or position. And, so, he went away sad. The way into the kingdom of God seems to be by dropping strength and following weakness.

Will It Work?

I cannot prove to you that Jesus will accept you should you come into his presence and let down your guard. I can tell you that the whole character of Jesus as we meet him in the gospels suggests this love. "Come to me, all who labor and are heavy laden, and I will give you rest," Jesus said (Matthew 11: 28). I can tell you, as well, that this love has been true for me and others, as it was true for the woman in the story. In Jesus' loving presence, we safely may drop our pretension of strength and admit our needy weakness.

You may need to do this kind of confession in the presence of another person in order to help you through the crisis of getting it out. Some will work through therapy, some with a spiritual counselor, some with a friend or in a small group. Some will just need to be quietly in the presence of God, on their knees or in the shower, on a walk or in a sanctuary.

However you come to it, such admission of sin and shame is the way to health. The popular wisdom is backwards when it denounces Christianity's emphasis on owning fault and admitting unworthiness. Honest confession does not produce a negative self-concept. A diminished self-image actually arises when we try to justify ourselves, when we confess on the surface without opening our souls. Then, when we try to be worthy, we feel forever unworthy. But when the walls finally break and we let our profound sense of shame and unworthiness flow out, God provides the grace that puts us together from the inside out.

> *In Jesus' loving presence, we may safely admit our needy weakness.*

That spring day years ago, my counselor brought me to forgiveness by accepting the worst I had to offer. The woman in our story was made whole because Jesus accepted her love. He did not blanch at her presence. He did not flinch at her touch, nor did he turn from her tears. He received her gift of love as she poured out her life. And by that accepting love, she was healed.

It took faith to go to a Pharisee's house in search of love. It takes faith, in the presence of all the voices that condemn us, to open up the old wounds before God. Jesus' love drew the woman there. His love draws us now. One inspires the other — faith and forgiving love. They circle around each other in glorious harmony. I wish you the courage to enter that loop and be swept up in the healing love of Jesus. The prayer in the Exercises section is meant to help you do that.

What's more, the Afterword contains the steps we may take to enter into a saving, intimate relationship with God through Jesus Christ.

QUESTIONS FOR REFLECTION

The story of the woman who anointed Jesus' feet is found in Luke 7:36-50.

+ What about Jesus in this story draws you to him?
+ We learned from this story that we are led into a deeper connection with God, not by our strengths, but by our weaknesses. Using that criterion, what areas in your life might be the leaders in your path to greater intimacy with God?
+ If you came and stood behind Jesus, over what would you weep?
+ What might inspire your love for him?
+ What part of you, like Simon the Pharisee, would be offended or embarrassed by your crying and your anointing of Jesus' feet?
+ In other words, what blocks your experience of forgiveness and the accompanying wholeness?
+ What could Jesus say that would effectively answer your "Simon?"
+ Jesus said to the woman, "Your faith has saved you; go in peace." If we only had this story to use, how would you define faith? Use as many concrete verbs and nouns as you can, in preference to abstract ideas.

Exercises

+ If you feel the desire to be joined to Jesus in a closer way, read the brief pages of the Afterword. Take time to work through the prayer at the end and make it your own.
+ The woman's alabaster flask was an extravagant gift of great worth, a gift of love, to be used all at once. What might be your alabaster flask? In other words what would you like to give Jesus as a gift of love? Try to find, make, write or draw some token that represents this gift.
+ Try on this Russian Orthodox prayer as a way of identifying with the woman in the story. Pray it daily this week:

O Lord, I know that I am not worthy nor sufficiently pleasing that Thou shouldst come under the roof of the house of my soul for it is entirely desolate and fallen in ruin and Thou wilt not find in me a place worthy to lay thy head. But as Thou didst humble thyself from on high for our sake, so now humble thyself to my lowliness. ...

As Thou didst not cast out the prostitute, the sinful woman who came to touch Thee, so have compassion on me a sinner who comes to touch Thee.

And as Thou didst not abhor the kiss of her sin-stained and unclean mouth, do not abhor my mouth, worse stained and more unclean than hers, nor my stained and shamed and unclean lips, nor still more my impure tongue.

But let the fiery coal of Thy most pure Body and Thy most precious Blood bring me sanctification, enlightenment and strengthening of my lowly soul and body, relief from the burden of my many transgressions.[1]

---

1   *The Divine Liturgy According to St. John Chrysostom* (South Canaan, Pa.; St. Tikhon's University Press; 1967) p. 97.

Chapter 8

TAKING A TOWEL AND A BASIN

John 13: 1-20

The account of the woman who anointed Jesus' feet led us to see that we connect most deeply with God when we offer him our woundedness. Coming into God's presence with openness and an honest reading of our lives is met with a response of forgiving grace. I am hopeful that, after reading these last three stories – the calling of the disciples, the question of the rich man, and the restoration of the sinful woman – you will have felt the urge to trust the Jesus you have met. I hope you will feel moved to release your life into his Father's care. When we do so, transformation follows. Through faith, we are joined to Jesus. Henceforth, God's Holy Spirit, the Spirit of Jesus, comes to dwell in us. As he does, the Spirit undertakes to make us more and more like the Jesus whom we have met and trusted. Our lives begin to change from the inside out. This is the wonderful, difficult, mystical adventure of life in Christ.

Such trust, of course, is not a one-time act that leads to a painless, finished transformation in us. God's desire is that we be in an eternal relationship of love with him. Like any relationship, love and trust deepen over time. They grow through the hundreds and thousands of little choices we make moment by moment. And there are bumps and setbacks along the way. Our life in Christ is one of process. We spiral in and out of desiring to be close to God and following his will. Some days, we come joyfully into God's presence with open hearts. Other days, we are highly reluctant even to pray. Such

> *Real faith in Christ finds tangible expression in daily life.*

undulations are normal. Over the long run, however, we become more like this Jesus whom we are learning to love. As resistance gives way to yielding and doubt to trust, we grow closer to the Father through knowing his Son Jesus Christ in the power and love of the Holy Spirit.

77

I cannot know how far along you are in your openness to awakening to God through discovering Jesus. Still, having considered the inner dynamics involved in our encountering Jesus, I would like to move to a consideration of how such faith and trust in Christ find tangible expressions in daily life. These next stories will be a preview of what Jesus asks from us if we go farther with him.

Our spiritual union with Christ will urge us to outward expression. Connecting with God inwardly demands, after the initial moments, a corresponding expression in the outer life. This, by no means, is automatic. Like everything else, outer change requires conscious intention. Entering loving communion with God our Father through his Son Jesus will move us to share that love. But if we are new at all this, we need to know what such love will look like and how we go about giving it.

In words, from the stories we have been studying, "Suppose you were to start down the road home, to drink living water, and to accept the call to follow Jesus wherever he goes, what would that look like, not just in terms of inner personal growth, but in the actual way you live your life?"

A Service to Be Passed Along

The gospel of John records an event that took place on the evening of the Last Supper , the night before Jesus died. John sets up the story within the drama of Jesus' final time with his disciples:

> Jesus knew that his hour had come to depart out of this world to the Father, having loved his own who were in the world, he loved them to the end. ... Jesus, knowing that the Father had given all things into his hands, and that he had come from God and was going back to God, rose from supper. He laid aside his outer garments, and taking a towel, tied it around his waist. Then he poured water into a basin and began to wash the disciples' feet and to wipe them with the towel that was wrapped around him.
>
> John 13:1-5

When Jesus came with the bowl to Simon Peter (the same disciple who had fallen on his knees in the boat during the great catch of fish), he initially was refused. Simon Peter could not bear to let Jesus wash his feet. This was the task of a servant, a menial job to cleanse the filth from feet that had been only clad in sandals during journeys along unpaved roads. Washing feet surely was beneath the man who had performed mighty miracles.

I wonder if this startling act of intimacy arose from what Jesus had experienced when the woman in our last chapter washed his feet with ointment and tears. Perhaps she had evoked for Jesus the power inherent in such a humble act.

> In the washing of the feet, Jesus undertook the menial task of a servant.

More passionately than any words, this visible service could communicate his love for his disciples.

After Jesus had overcome Simon Peter's reluctance and had washed all of the disciples' feet, he put on his robe and went back to the table. Then, he spoke to them of the meaning of his actions:

> Do you understand what I have done to you? You call me Teacher and Lord, and you are right, for so I am. If I, then, your Lord and Teacher, have washed your feet, you also ought to wash one another's feet. For I have given you an example that you also should do just as I have done to you. Truly, truly, I say to you, a servant is not greater than his master, nor is a messenger greater than the one who sent him. If you know these things, blessed are you if you do them.
>
> John 13:12-17

The repetition in Jesus' words leaves little room for doubt. Three times, Jesus told them that they should wash one another's feet. He says it concretely; he gave the literal example to be followed. Of course, further on we will consider this passage in its metaphorical meanings. But first, it is crucial to see that the physical act carries the meaning most effectively.

The Care of Feet

I have worked with this passage in several groups. Quite consistently, most people are uncomfortable with the thought of the literal washing of feet. This very resistance can be illuminating. Before we ever actually enact this ritual, we can understand the quality of relationships Jesus is commanding by exploring what is unsettling in the concrete act. Sticking with the physical dimension of the story, before spiritualizing it, can reveal the deeper spiritual meanings more clearly.

Near the beginning of my ministry in one congregation, I explored this passage with the leaders of the church. The study was a prelude to a retreat that might include the washing of feet. They tried on the idea of actually doing it. At the study, I asked them questions about their preconceptions of what the washing of feet would mean: If the thought of washing someone's feet makes you uncomfortable, what in particular do you think creates the difficulty? What quality of relationships is required to enact a ritual so intimate? What would have to change, in you and in our relationships with one another, in order to make doing this service a greater possibility?

The officers answered candidly with responses such as these: "We would need to be vulnerable with each other." "We would have to put aside thinking about ourselves for awhile to focus on each other." "We would have to be courageous; we would have to have faith that God wanted us to do this so we would be able to get through it." "We would have to be willing to let our relationships go beneath the surface, to a different level than we usually interact on." "We would have to risk being embarrassed around each other." "We would need love."

On the retreat, enough people had responded favorably that I decided to risk offering a foot-washing ceremony as a voluntary worship service. Right to the last minute, the bulk of the officers debated whether or not to participate. As the hour came, they decided to risk it.

As nervous as we all were, we arranged the room to minimize the discomfort. Someone lowered the lights. Someone else made sure the doors were shut so passersby would not intrude. Soft music soothed the awkward silences between the sounds of the splashing water. And then, after reading the passage together, one by one these upper middle-class, frightened, reserved church officers knelt in front of each other. Shoes were unlaced and gently removed, the precious foot ladled with warm water and toweled off. Twenty minutes passed as each washed and in turn received the washing.

The washing of feet means our relationships go beneath the surface.

Afterward, most of them said it was much easier to wash someone's feet than to have your feet washed. The active washing gives you something to do. You maintain some control over the experience. By force of will, you can overcome convention and care for the other's feet. But when your feet are washed, you only can receive. The warm water and the soft touch feel very good, but it is hard to accept the gift that someone is stooping to bathe your feet, as unique and embarrassing and worn as they may be! When it is over, though, feelings of affection arise. What a tender act, that someone would take off my shoes, rinse and dry my feet. The experience was humbling for everyone.

> 'If we can wash someone's feet, we can do anything God asks us!'

The effect was a great release of joy and energy within the group. Our relationships deepened, and a shared commitment to faith grew among the officers. As someone said, "If we can wash someone's feet, we can do anything else God asks us!"

Quality of Relationships

Having briefly explored the story literally, what does it say to us symbolically? How will followers of Jesus enact the washing of feet in their everyday lives? The meaning, of course, goes far deeper than the single act. The washing of feet becomes a paradigm for relationships between those who actively are reconnecting with God. Washing someone's feet means tending to an exposed, humbled part of that person. It means taking gentle care of what a person offers to show us. All the while, we know that what we are doing in caring for "feet" is at once very difficult and very comforting for the recipient.

> The washing of feet means taking gentle care of what a person offers to show us.

Allowing *our* feet to be washed means revealing to another person a part of us most often kept hidden and protected. It means risking the sight, smell and feel of our feet before another person. Effort is needed to receive their ministrations; humility is required to relax enough to be soothed by the gift, as our washer desires us to be. We are showing a secret side of ourselves and accepting another's care.

It is very difficult to feel superior to someone whose feet you have washed. It is difficult to ignore or put down someone who recently has washed your feet. The interaction between people changes in the intimacy of such an activity.

Thinking of the story in this way, it becomes evident what kind of relationships Jesus expected his followers to have. He desires that we relate to one another with increasing honesty and tender regard. We have noted that our spiritual growth means a greater knowledge of self in concert with a greater knowledge of God. Just so, revealing our "feet" to others and tending to the "feet" they show to us leads to deepening our union with Christ.

Meant for Communion, Not Pseudo-Community

We considered the individual lives of the characters in our previous stories. But, of course, no one lives as a solitary individual. God made us to have our lives in relationship to others. Our relationships are an essential aspect of what makes us who we are. The people we have been reading about had family and community contexts. The younger and elder brother did not relate to their father in isolation. Their relationship as brothers was a powerful force in the story. Simon Peter, James and John left more than their nets on the beach to follow Jesus. They shifted family contexts, leaving home to become part of a new family centered on Jesus. The sinful woman is only understood in relation to the entire community of which she was a part. So, the story of the washing of the feet confirms the importance Jesus placed on our relationships – not just as individuals with God, but also with one another in a shared life of commitment to Christ. The call to love God is inseparable from the command to love others. God's purpose is an intimate fellowship of brothers and sisters who recognize one heavenly Father through being united in his Son Jesus. We are joined together by the bond of the Holy Spirit who dwells in each of us individually yet, in doing so, makes us members of one another.

Unfortunately, however, many of us have not experienced such mystical communion within the context of the church, the community where such foot-washing love is supposed to be normal. Sadly, too often churches exhibit what M. Scott Peck defined as "pseudo-community."[1] People get along on the surface. They profess to care for each other. Socially, they interact. But rarely do the relationships go deeper than ordinary exchanges.

I once asked a woman who had not been to church for several months if she wouldn't like to come back and join the fellowship. Her reply exposed our pseudo-community all too clearly. She said, "I've just felt too awful to be with all those happy faces."

Is that what we've become? Have churches become a place where you have to get your life together in order to present a successful appearance? Aren't churches supposed to be a fellowship of the broken who are leading each other to the healing source, of helping each other get the messes cleaned up, of sinners who share the grace of Christ? Jesus gave his disciples the ritual of the washing of feet in order that the church might be a place of tender, intimate care. When hurting people have to put on a smiley face to come to church, somehow we have lost the meaning of the washing of feet.

---

1   Peck, M. Scott; *The Different Drum* (New York; Simon and Schuster; 1988) p. 86.

The Basement and the Sanctuary

In many churches these days, Twelve Step groups are meeting in basements or tucked-away classrooms. These groups are based on the kind of open fellowship inaugurated by Jesus' washing of the feet. Throughout the course of a meeting, participants share their struggles with alcoholism, food addictions, sexual abuse, or any of many other debilitating behaviors that

> The call to love God is inseparable from the command to love others.

may be the focus of a particular meeting. They offer each other dirty feet and receive humble tending from each other. The group offers the safety of anonymity to participants; a consistent, uplifting support; and an understanding forgiveness of failures. In addition, these fellowships refer to the Twelve Steps, a list of principles that includes a firm reliance on a Higher Power to transform those aspects of life over which we are powerless.

The Twelve Step groups are attempting to live out the very kind of spirituality we have been describing in these pages. The Christians who worship upstairs in the sanctuaries could learn quite a bit from their partners in the basement. At the same time, participants in Twelve Step programs provided me with much of the inspiration for this

> The sanctuary and the basement can be brought closer together.

work. Many have told me how they long for more Christ-content than their meetings provide. They want more than a generic spirituality. They desire to re-enter Christian faith, and discover how the stories of Jesus relate to their newfound honesty and vulnerability.

Both groups could learn from each other. How wonderful it would be if the basement and the sanctuary were brought closer together. I am hopeful that Jesus' gift of the foot-washing ritual can be recovered – at both the literal and symbolic level – to help us move in that direction. The growth of interest in home groups for study, prayer, accountability and support is very encouraging. In fact, I hope that even now you are reading in preparation to discuss this story with others.

The Washing of Feet

Reconnecting with God is an intensely personal activity. Much of it has to be done alone. We need enough silence to hear what God is saying to us from his Word. Space apart from the demands of the world is necessary for us to get in touch with our yearning for God and to make our way home.

At the same time, we cannot reconnect without other people. God has made us to interact with one another. For many people, confession only can occur if there is a ready ear to hear. We need the help of others to make sense of our thoughts and to sort out our feelings. Most of us benefit from direction in the interpretation of Bible stories. Many of the moments crucial to my own growth have occurred in conversations of foot-washing quality with other people.

As you grow in your relationship with God our heavenly Father, it is essential to be in relationship with other people on a similar journey. We need each other to keep up our courage, to expose our rationalizations and to affirm our progress. We worship, not only in private, but also together with other followers of Jesus. We study, not just alone, but also with others to gain new perspectives and share our unique insights.

So, I will recommend that you get involved in a church if you are not already. Once in a church, I will say straightforwardly that many of your interactions might be disappointing. Our churches are full of pseudo-community, and full of people who are frightened to take the stories of Jesus personally and seriously. The fact that you are consciously on a spiritual quest makes you different from the majority of people. A certain amount of loneliness can be expected.

At the same time, God never leaves us alone. There are people in every place who make it a priority to live in conscious union with Jesus. In fact, as you awaken more and more to life in Christ, you will find those people who are on a similar journey. Sometimes, it will seem as if they are appearing from out of nowhere. Where once you thought you were alone, soon you will find help in the most unexpected places. God will meet our needs for spiritual interaction with others. There is a small group with room for you.

> *Others are depending on us to grow closer to God.*

Jesus' command to wash feet, though, makes some requirements of us as well. Reconnecting with our heavenly Father through his Son Jesus is not for our personal benefit alone. As individuals, we may decide we can live with misery on certain days and simply not pursue serving God. After all, "It's my life." But the truth is that others are depending on us to grow closer to God through knowing Jesus so that we may be of some aid to them. What we learn in reconnecting with God is meant to be shared in love with others.

Those who seriously take Jesus' command to wash feet will look for tired, hurting feet among those they meet. Not just literally, of course. But as we listen, and grow more sensitive, we can apprehend when others are hurting. Many will expose a bit of their pain to see how we respond. We can grow in our ability to make inquiries about other's lives. The basin of warm water to soothe aching muscles is offered every time we ask to listen to another person's story. Our compassion is a soft towel as we treat another person's feet, their exposed and embarrassing aspects, as a precious treasure.

Along the way of following Jesus, we will try to deepen the interactions we have with other people. We can take the risk by exposing more of ourselves than we usually do. We, so to speak, can offer our feet. Every interaction is a chance to show forth love. Many encounters include an opportunity to take the conversation deeper. We can practice going down into the ache of life instead of always trying to be "up" in the forced hilarity of our culture.

The heart of God was revealed in the washing of feet. During the night, when the powers of darkness were riding the winds, when urgency would have driven most of us to a frenzy, Jesus slowly, deliberately washed the feet of each disciple. When he had only one evening left to teach them the essence of his desire for them, Jesus washed his disciple's feet.

> *The heart of God was revealed in the washing of feet.*

In Chapter Ten, we will more fully explore what it means that Jesus gave his life for us. For now, we see that whenever we would hesitate to live with a foot-washing quality for others, we can draw strength from Jesus' own actions, and his words, "So if I, your Lord and Teacher, have washed your feet, you also ought to wash one another's feet."

Questions for Reflection

The story of the washing of feet is found in John 13:1-20.

+ What are some ways, besides literally, that we both wash other people's feet and have our feet washed?
+ How would you say Jesus has washed your feet?
+ What, in your experience of the love of Jesus, forms the basis for washing other people's feet?
+ How does this kind of service link us to Christ? What would need to change in our relationships with others in order to make enacting the washing of feet a greater possibility?
+ How have aspects of the church blocked the caliber of relationship demanded by the washing of feet?

- In churches you have seen, what activities, structures, programs, or attitudes help to promote relationships of "foot-washing" quality?
- Who are the people in your life with whom you come closest to having this kind of relationship? What new risks of love might you be called to take as a result of your spiritual growth?

Exercises

- Conduct a week-long experiment during which time you will try to note where in conversations you could take things to a deeper level. Try, if you are able, in compassion to make inquiries about another person's life, to risk going down into pain and avoid going up into superficiality. Each evening, make notes on your progress, the reactions of others and the degree of risk required.
- If you are in a small group, consider actually conducting the washing of feet. I have seen it work well when the group first reads and discusses the passage. We usually arrange chairs in a circle, and play a tape of soft, meditative music. Then, working with two basins and towels, the first two participants kneel before two others. We stress that anyone has the right to decline participation simply by shaking their head if someone comes to them. If there is agreement, however, the washers take off the shoes of the people who are sitting. Then, with first one foot and then the other over the bowl, the washer ladles the feet with warm water. Then, the washers towel off the feet and pass the towel to the person sitting and go back to their own chairs. This continues until everyone has washed another's feet once and have had their own feet washed once.
- Try on the following prayer:

> Jesus, come, my feet are dirty. You have become a servant for my sake, so fill your basin with water; come, wash my feet. I know that I am bold in saying this, but your own words have made me fearful: "If I do not wash your feet, you will have no companionship with me." Wash my feet, then, so that I may be your companion. But what am I saying, "Wash my feet?" Peter could say these words, for all that needed washing were his feet. For the rest, he was completely clean. I must be made clean with that other washing of which you said: "I have a baptism with which I must be baptized."[1]

---

1   Origen; from *A Triduum Sourcebook*; Huck, Gabe; Simcoe, Mary Anne; editors (Chicago; Archdiocese of Chicago; 1983) p. 10.

Chapter 9

THE FACE THAT IS EVERYWHERE

Matthew 25:31-46

The last public teaching of Jesus recorded in the gospel of Matthew is a provocative parable about the day of judgment. Jesus said that, at the end of time, he – the Son of Man – will be seated on a throne of glory. All people will be gathered before him. And then, with the authority of a king and the calling of a shepherd, Jesus will separate people into two groups, the sheep and the goats. To the ones designated as sheep, the king will set forth his reasons for a good judgment:

> Come, you who are blessed by my Father, inherit the kingdom prepared for you from the foundation of the world. For I was hungry and you gave me food, I was thirsty, and you gave me drink, I was a stranger and you welcomed me, I was naked and you clothed me, I was sick and you visited me, I was in prison and you came to me.
>
> Matthew 25:34-37

In the parable, Jesus said that the righteous will inquire about when they had ever seen their Lord in such states as hunger, illness or imprisonment. Then, Jesus said he will make the startling reply, "Truly, I say to you, as you did it to one of the least of these my brothers, you did it to me."

In the parable, the king will go on to curse the unrighteous for failing to give him drink, to welcome him, to clothe him, and so on. In shock at their offense, they will ask when they ever could have been guilty of such horrible neglect. The answer will be chilling: "Truly, I say to you, as you did not do it to one of the least of these, you did not do it to me."

Parables concern the way we live right now.

We may well be shocked that it was Jesus himself who spoke so pointedly about eternal judgment. He confirmed that the issue of the wrath of a loving, yet just, God is an important one. We will consider it further in the next chapter. Our focus now, however, is not future judgment, but what Jesus asks of us in this present life. The force of this parable actually concerns the way we live *right now*. As they are told, parables are meant to inspire a change in thought or action. Hopefully, over the course of this study, we have entered into a deeper relationship with Jesus. Now, the words of this one we have come to trust can energize us to refocus the very way we look at others and act toward them.

In the account of the washing of the feet, Jesus three times repeated his command that the disciples wash one another's feet. Given the economical writing style in the Bible, such repetition signals an important and unmistakable imperative. In this parable of the sheep and goats, Jesus repeated his list four times. There could be no doubt in his audience of what he was trying to say.

How we treat others is how we are treating Jesus! When we give food to someone who is hungry, we are giving it to Jesus. If we ignore someone who is thirsty, we have denied Jesus a drink. Welcoming a stranger with open arms is embracing our Lord himself. But sizing up someone, dismissing their importance and turning away is equivalent to dispensing with Jesus.

Jesus left his disciples with standing orders for how to live after his departure. They were, and are, to love him by loving others. The church has followed Christ's intent in its long history of compassion. Hospitals, schools, shelters, hospices, clothes closets, Habitat for Humanity, orphanages, food pantries and hundreds of other ministries have been started through the centuries in Jesus' name. As we grow in being followers of Jesus, we discover that our relationship to Jesus includes caring for the least of these. If we want to touch him, to be near him, to show love for him, we do so or fail to do so by our actions toward the least.

> How we treat others is how we are treating Jesus!

At first, this may seem overwhelming. Indeed, this is one of the most challenging of his teachings. It's exhausting to think that about five billion people live on Earth. If all of them are, in effect, Jesus, and if any of them is in need, I am hopelessly behind and doomed to be one of the goats. This parable, then, becomes not motivating, but humiliating.

Several important considerations, however, can help us tap into this teaching as a wellspring for replenishing our acts of compassion:

1) We may understand that the parable uses *hyperbole*. The force of its message was to wake us up to the reality that the least little one is worthy of our care; in the most obscure and undesirable, there is Jesus waiting to be loved.

Of course, we cannot succeed every time. God knows that we cannot be perfect. We do not instantly become "goats" because of our past, or even future, neglects. The parable is intended to motivate us now to begin seeing others with the same affection we have for Jesus.

2) We may realize that *not every person in the world is or can be our responsibility*. Many of us, to be sure, are not acting on behalf of others anywhere near our capacity. Some of us are overworked and approaching burnout. Morton Kelsey, an Episcopal minister and author who exhibited a rich compassion to all he encountered, made this observation. He likened our call to love to picking up bundles. No one can pick up all the bundles in the world. *The key is to find those bundles with our names on them.* We strive to discern which people are our bundles and which are not. When we are comfortable that we are tending to the bundles God has given us, we may leave the rest in God's care.[1]

3) *We love the least by drawing on our love for Jesus.* Considering the "least of these" as if they were Jesus need not make us feel guilty that we do not love them more. Rather, we may use this idea to fuel our imaginations and thereby inspire our love. If we have met Jesus in the story of the woman at the well, we have felt love swell in us for this one who knows us so completely and, yet, loves us anyway. In the story of the rich man, we may have felt relief that Jesus does not mean for us to play the world's game and succeed in all the wrong places.

> *The key is to find those bundles with our names on them.*

We can love him with our whole heart. The sinful woman found forgiveness and, entering that story, we, too, may have felt the healing of old wounds. In all these stories, Jesus elicits love from us. He draws us to him; his compassion sparks our devotion. We may transfer our feelings of affection for Jesus onto those in the world whom we otherwise would consider least. Our love for Jesus can lead us. By loving them, we are loving him.

---

1   Kelsey, Morton; "Healing and Love;" lecture at Stony Point Conference Center, New York; May 1988.

Who Are The Least?

Who are the brothers of Jesus, even the least of whom he sends us to love? My interpretation of this passage is that he means every person. It is true that not everyone is yet joined to Jesus through faith. Though all of us are children of God by creation, not all are yet children of God by adoption into Christ the Son of God. In fact, one of the main purposes of this book is to invite readers into that life-giving, life-transforming relationship with Christ. My ardent desire is that people come to know God as their beloved Father through meeting his Son Jesus Christ in the mystical bond of the Holy Spirit.

Now, while I know that not every person has entered such a union, I am yet called to love each as a brother of Jesus. Not because of what people have done to show faith, but because of what Jesus has done. The eternal Son of God became a human being in Jesus. God "brothered" us in the person of Jesus. By entering the world, Jesus entered a kinship with all people. He was made like we are. So, he has come to share in our humanity. Thus, every person from high to low, from unbeliever to saint, is related to God in two ways:

> God "brothered" us in the person of Jesus.

1) God is our creator and the one who upholds our lives even now.

2) In Jesus, God is our brother in the flesh.

Jesus sends us to love all those whom he has made his brothers and sisters by sharing in their humanity. Whether or not they have answered his call to follow him, to drink living water, to come into the party, does not affect his sending of me to love them.

Now, which of these brothers and sisters of Jesus fits the category of the *least* may range broadly. Of course, the faraway poor come to mind, those who are strangers to our Western comforts and economies. There also are the near-poor, dwelling on the broken streets I have learned to avoid. They live in chaos behind ramshackle walls in parts of town I pretend don't exist. Out of sight and out of mind. But even closer to daily life, the "least" simply may be the person whom other people avoid. At work, there are some "least of these" who perhaps bear the brunt of coffee hour chatter. Families may spawn someone who becomes the least of these as an object of blame for the family's problems. The least of these show up in churches, clubs and parties as the ones who too obviously are needy of attention, too vocal, too different from the rest.

We can be honest enough to admit that, personally, the least of these for us are probably the people we "least" want to be around. My grandmother instilled in me a passion to wash my hands and stay clean, along with a concomitant fear of hospitals and sick people. Even as I worked on these pages, someone across the plane sneezed and I involuntarily recoiled! Loud, abrasive people become the least for me. I steer around them as much as possible

> We can begin to look at others with a spiritually romantic imagination.

– unless I can think of a safe, anonymous way to deflate them. People on the discard pile of human preference also become the least of these. The woman reaching out to me in the nursing home hallway with open mouth and vacant eyes sends shivers down my spine. Or, I simply, cruelly, block out of my mind the children living in dysfunction and neglect minutes from my home. For all kinds of the least of these, I do not know what to say to their pain. I do not know how to act in the face of their need. I have no solutions to their poverty and I cannot solve them. They are the "least of these" and I can't seem to help it. The "least of these" are all over the place, wherever people are reduced, dismissed, shunned or avoided.

The raw truth is that many people who feel undesirable to us always will seem that way. Obnoxious people more than likely will remain obnoxious. Sick people will not stop being ill just so we can have an easier time visiting them. Prisoners not often will have troubled pasts transformed into bright futures. Some people always will be scary. It takes a long time for misfits to fit.

Yet, each one of them is a brother of Jesus. What I do or don't do to the "least of these" I do or don't do to him. The force of the parable is inescapable. A life that is reconnected with God through our encounters with Jesus needs to find expressions of Christ's compassion. We have seen throughout this study that God our Father pours forth the waters of his love to heal us. But we are not to let those waters grow stagnant. God's love is meant to flow through us to others. As Jesus offers us so much life, he also asks us to respond with a dedication of our lives to follow him and a new intention to relate to others with compassion. As we saw in the last chapter, we seek to develop relationships of foot-washing intimacy. But how can we learn to love those whom we have personally identified as the "least of these?"

Learning To Love The 'Least Of These'

We can begin to look at others with a spiritually romantic imagination. Knowing full well that the person is not literally Jesus, we pretend. I look at the one in the bed and say, "There is Jesus. I love Jesus and so I will love this one." The loud person goes into his needy tirade. Instead of turning away, I can use imagination. There is Jesus; he is lonesome and needy in that person. I can welcome him. I pick up the phone and call someone who is grieving, even though I am already tired, because on the other end of the line is Jesus who once wept when he lost his friend. Because Jesus is our brother, we visualize his sharing in every human experience. By the extension of our imagination, we see him in the condition and situation of everyone whom we meet.

Amazingly, looked at in this way, we begin to see people differently. The "least of these" are elevated from that dreadful category. It is a moving experience to suddenly see in the incoherent expression of a woman in a nursing home the Christ who has loved me so much. She gains more worth in my perception than I would have thought possible and, so, my attitude and actions toward her change, as well. I need no longer see the man who wanders off the street with decades of tangled problems as a nuisance to be gotten rid of as quickly as possible. Rather, he offers a way for me to show affection to my Lord. Reading to a child at an elementary school full of at-risk children can be a way to give attention to Jesus. In these ways and many more, the "least of these" are transformed in our perception. We love Christ more deeply through the gift of being able to care for Christ through them. This change occurs not by guilty, straining compulsion, but through the joyful romance of my feelings for Jesus.

Overcoming Difficulty

Sometimes, of course, our imaginations may wilt at seeing Jesus in some people. The violence, the self-centeredness, the distortions of addiction, the ravages of illness may daunt us. We may feel that the person of Jesus and the forcefully apparent faults of the "least of these" are in contradiction. We mentally know that we are called to treat each one as we would treat Jesus, whom we have grown to love. But no love is being inspired in us.

In such times, I have found it helpful to reverse the imagery. I strive not to see Jesus in the person, but to see the person through Jesus' eyes. He was able to deal with self-righteous Pharisees, people possessed by demons, weasels in business, the morally compromised and even the fearfully diseased. So, if I can link myself with the stories of Jesus' interactions with people, I can be moved along with compassion I don't naturally possess.

In riding up in an elevator to visit someone gravely ill, for example, I may be suddenly struck with the force of my background. I am repulsed. There is no way I can go and smell that disease, look at the feeding tube, or clasp that limp hand. I want to slip a card under the door and run. But, sometimes, I can lay hold of a story of Jesus and find strength. I can recall that Jesus did not turn away from the man who had lived among the tombs. That man was bruised with open sores, naked, unwashed and howling. Jesus received him and made him well. In the name of that Jesus, then, I will go into this room and receive the ill one whom I find.

To illustrate this further, I may be preparing for an encounter with someone I detest because he refuses to examine his life. He consistently avoids being responsible for his growth, and then wonders why he has so many problems. It is helpful, then, to remember the woman at the well. I see Jesus speaking with her under the hot sun. He invites her to consider her past. He tells the truth about her mistakes and does not get taken in by her attempts to deflect the conversation. Neither, though, does he consider her sins to be fatal. He offers her in that moment his healing acceptance. So, in the name of that Jesus, I will meet this man. I will go with honesty and with mercy, praying for the wisdom of Jesus to hold the two in balance. Remembering the story where Jesus once met me, I claim Jesus' compassion as my own.

Jesus' parable of the sheep and the goats is meant to jar us. He wants us to see the inseparable connection between our relationship with him and our compassion toward others. He worked in our lives when we were but the "least of these." He sends us to them in whatever form they may appear. We go, knowing that we cannot pick up every bundle. We just have to look for the ones with our names on them, the people whom God brings in our path. Then, we seek to relate to them by using our imaginations. We see Jesus in their life situations. We have met Jesus through the stories of the gospels. Now, we are sent to enact compassion to others, even the "least of these," as if each one were Jesus. In this way, our union with Christ will grow even deeper.

QUESTIONS FOR REFLECTION

The parable of the sheep and goats may be found in Matthew 25:31-46.

+ What does it mean to be one of the "least?"
+ What is annoying about the "least?" What don't you like about them?
+ In what situations do you find Jesus hungry, sick, in prison, a stranger, naked and thirsty? Can you name the "least of these" who are in your community?

Your church? Your workplace or school? Your family?

+ How could thinking of each of the "least of these" as *being Jesus* help your interaction with them?
+ Why do you think Jesus was so serious about this?
+ What accounts of Jesus' dealing with others could be helpful to the way you deal with the "least of these?"

Exercises

+ Close your eyes and wait quietly for some of the "least of these" whom you recently have encountered to appear in your mind.
+ See them there. See Jesus in each one. Then ask yourself: "What tangible expression of compassion could I perform for each one? Can I imagine doing it out of love for Jesus? Am I willing to do it?"
+ Nearly 500 years ago, George Herbert described the life of a country pastor in terms still applicable to all of us today. Herbert recognized our call to the "least of these:"

> He holds the rule, that nothing is little in God's service; if it once have the honour of that Name it grows instantly. Wherefore neither disdaineth he to enter into the poorest cottage, though he even creep into it and though it smell never so loathsomely. For both God is there also and those for whom God died.[1]

Consider to which "cottages" God may be calling you to go. Imagine how, even among the least desirable people, you will find God there and those for whom God died.

+ Meditate on this ancient prayer of Celtic hospitality:

> I saw a stranger yestreen,
> I put food in the eating place,
> Drink in the drinking place,

---

1   Herbert, George; *The Complete English Poems*; Tobin, John; ed. (London; Penguin Books; 1991) p. 224.

Music in the listening place,
And in the sacred name of the Triune,
  He blessed myself and my house
My cattle and my dear ones,
  And the lark said in her song
      Often, often, often,
Goes the Christ in the stranger's guise.[1]

1   Macleod, Kenneth; from an Iona Community postcard.

Chapter 10

THE CUP OF BLESSING

Mark 10:35-45; Mark 14:22-25; 36

Imagine Jesus sitting at a table, inviting you to come and sit before him. In the center of the table is a chalice. It is the cup of the world's pain, rage, regret and sin. He invites you to pour your share into the cup. Without a word, you agree. Dark liquid comes spilling from your mouth. Mistakes, moments of cruelty, seasons of sorrow — and even your guilt — flow into the cup. You can hardly believe there is room enough in the chalice for it all. You are ashamed of the volume of the deep, brownish-red bile. Jesus waits while it all spills out of you. Then, he looks you in the eyes. He wants to drink this cup. You can hardly believe the request. But he insists and you nod shyly. Jesus picks up the cup and drains it. You see by his face that the taste is bitter and the effect is dire. He shudders, but continues to drink. He does not stop until the last drop is gone.

Jesus again looks in your eyes as he places the cup on the table. He slides it across. The cup has been refilled. The wine is red, but pure and fine. "Drink this," he says. "This is my blood poured out for you for the forgiveness of sins."

You take the chalice. The cup of judgment has become the cup of blessing. The wine fills you with warmth. You feel cleansed. Free. Energized, as if with new life.

When you have finished, Jesus reaches across the table and embraces you. He blesses you and then sends you back out to your life. As you go, he reminds you always to care for his little ones.

Could such an exchange be possible?

This, in fact, is the essence of why Jesus came to us.

In this chapter, we journey into the mystery of the cup Jesus drank and the cup he gives to us.

The Ultimate Reversal

All through these pages, we have been considering Jesus' encounters with the people he met. We have listened to what he taught and have seen how he drew others into a healing, forgiving relationship with his heavenly Father. Jesus then sent those who belonged to him to love even the least and the lost with his foot-washing kind of love. Hopefully, we have entered the gospel stories in such a way that we have found our own lives written there. Through meeting Jesus as he met individuals, we have been invited to be reconnected to God.

Now, we will turn to the meaning of Jesus' life and death as a whole. If we have felt his tender love, we may be shocked to realize how many people rejected Jesus. His own close friends deserted him. Those who hailed him as king one day turned and shouted for his death just a few days later. The most religious of his people found him the most offensive.

The gospel of John says: "The true light which enlightens every one, was coming into the world ... yet the world did not know him. He came to his own, and his own people did not receive him" (John 1:9-11). He later explains that, "The light has come into the world, and people loved the darkness rather than the light because their deeds were evil" (John 3:19). We have noted throughout our study the resistance to God that is within us. Sometimes, the conflict can be acute. We grieve to discover how often we choose the dry desert of self-will over the living water Christ Jesus offers. We blush to realize how brazenly we reject Jesus by disdaining the least of his brothers. We know what makes for life and, yet, we choose what leads to spiritual death. The crowd that turned on Jesus includes us.

Yet, God anticipated the rejection of Jesus, and even planned for it! The coming of Jesus includes one surprise after another about the nature of God. But none is bigger than this: God took the death of Jesus and made it his triumph over our sin and evil.

> *God anticipated the rejection of Jesus, and even planned for it!*

The crucifixion of Jesus in utter humiliation and pain became the foundation of God's victory. The very act that most shames us – our betrayal of Jesus who came to love us – became the basis for everlasting forgiveness and life.

To put it plainly, God scooped us! He pulled the ultimate switcheroo. What should have damned us instead became the basis of our eternal salvation. During the days of Jesus on Earth, the cross was the gruesome symbol of the most brutal death yet devised. Now, it is the symbol of life. It had meant utter rejection. Now, it means glorious reconciliation.

Why Jesus Came

In Mark 10, the same chapter in which we read of Jesus' blessing the children and his encounter with the rich young ruler, we also find a rather audacious request by two of Jesus' disciples.

James and John anticipated that Jesus was the long-awaited Messiah who very soon would restore the nation of Israel to a place of glory. He would take his place as king and, in this way, God himself would be enthroned over the whole world, setting all things right. The two brothers asked Jesus if they could sit, one at his right hand and one at his left, when he entered heaven and took this seat of triumph. With such hubris, the young men showed they had little understanding of why Jesus had come.

Jesus asked them, "Are you able to drink the cup that I drink, or to be baptized with the baptism with which I am baptized?" In other words, Jesus asked them if they were prepared to go through what he would go through. Since they still didn't get it, he gave them a succinct summary of his entire mission in the world: "But whoever would be great among you must be your servant, and whoever would be first among you must be slave of all. For the Son of Man came not to be served but to serve, and to give his life as a ransom for many."

Jesus came to give his life away. We understand this on two levels. First, Jesus gave himself through the constant service of forgiving, healing love toward those he met. We have seen this throughout these pages. Second, Jesus would give up his life on the cross and, in so doing, free us from our bondage to sin and separation from God.

The rest of the New Testament picks up this paradoxical theme that Jesus' death brings us life. Feel the power in the words of the Apostle Paul, who particularly stressed this in his letters:

> The saying is trustworthy and deserving of full acceptance, that Christ Jesus came into the world to save sinners, of whom I am the foremost (I Timothy 1:15).
>
> Grace to you and peace from God our Father and the Lord Jesus Christ, who gave himself for our sins to deliver us from the present evil age (Galatians 1:3, 4).
>
> God shows his love for us in that while we were still sinners, Christ died for us. ... For if while we were enemies we were reconciled to God by the death of his Son, much more, now

that we are reconciled, shall we be saved by his life (Romans 5: 8, 10).

But now in Christ Jesus you who once were far off have been brought near by the blood of Christ (Ephesians 2:13).

For the word of the cross is folly to those who are perishing, but to us who are being saved it is the power of God. ... For the foolishness of God is wiser than men, and the weakness of God is stronger than men. ... For I decided to know nothing among you except Jesus Christ and him crucified (1 Corinthians 1:18, 25; 2:2).

Jesus came to save us from the sin that separated us from God and caused all manner of distortion in our lives. He reconciled us to his heavenly Father so that we can know God in the same intimate way that he does.

But how could the death of Jesus be our life? How could our rejection of Christ be the means that God forgave all our sins? The phrasing is so simple: Christ came to save sinners; his death on the cross brought us forgiveness. But the depths of meaning in these words are unfathomable.

In these next few pages, we will attempt to approach the meaning of the cross, not directly, but through another potent symbol that Jesus used in our story from Mark – the *cup*.

The Third Cup of the Night

On his last night with his disciples, perhaps after he washed their feet, Jesus celebrated with them the traditional Jewish feast of Passover. On that evening, people gathered as families in their homes to recall the story of the Exodus, the calling forth of God's people from slavery in Egypt. The meal was highly ritualized, from each item of food and drink to the prayers said throughout the feast. The head of the family had a sacred form to follow. At every Passover, there were (and still are) four cups of red wine to be shared during the course of the meal. These four cups correspond to the four-fold promise that God gave to his people while they groaned under Egyptian rule.

In Exodus 6, we read how the LORD[1] spoke to Moses, the leader whom he had raised up:

> I have heard the groaning of the people of Israel whom the Egyptians hold as slaves, and I have remembered my covenant. Say therefore to the people of Israel,
> I am the LORD, and I will bring you out from under the burdens of the Egyptians, and
> I will deliver you from slavery to them, and
> I will redeem you with an outstretched arm and with great acts of judgment.
> I will take you to be my people, and I will be your God, and you shall know that I am the LORD your God.

During the Passover feast, the first two cups were blessed and shared before the main meal of bitter herbs, stewed fruit and roasted lamb. After the dinner, the father would lift the third cup and repeat the third part of the LORD's four-fold promise: I will redeem you with an outstretched arm and great acts of judgment.

> *To redeem means to save someone.*

The father would say the prescribed prayer of thanks, then pass around the third cup. As they partook, the people would recall what their God had done to save them.

This third cup was the cup of redemption. To *redeem* means to save someone by getting them out of one situation and into another. By an act on one person's part, another person is set free from a desperate plight, whether it be slavery, widowhood, capture or some other binding fate.

The LORD redeemed his people from slavery in Egypt by sending 10 consecutive plagues upon the Pharaoh, who repeatedly refused to let Israel's people go. The last plague, the slaying of the first born, finally broke the king's will. Pharaoh set the Israelites free. But even as they left, Pharaoh changed his mind and ordered his armies to give chase. At the shores of the Red Sea, the LORD

---

1   The use of a small font and all caps in "LORD" renders the Hebrew letters for YHWH, the sacred name of God first given to his people in Exodus 3. YHWH is translated as "I Am Who I Am." I find it important to preserve the use of LORD because this is the name God has given us and we are ever reminded that the God who is the Father of our Lord Jesus Christ is not some generic god or lord but is *the* LORD, one God, Father, Son and Holy Spirit.

God parted the waters for the fleeing Hebrews and then closed the waters over the pursuing Egyptians. By a mighty act, God's people were liberated, but their oppressors were destroyed. The cup of redemption for the Hebrews was a cup of judgment for the Egyptians.

It was at this climactic point in the recollection of the sacred story that *Jesus interrupted the traditional order!* He added his own words about the cup. Looking at the red wine remaining in the shared goblet he said, "This is my blood of the covenant, which is poured out for many" (Mark 14:24). The cup of judgment became the cup of Jesus' blood poured out. In the Passover feast, the judgment of God was described as the destruction of the Egyptian army. Now, we are to think of God's act of judgment as the offering of Jesus' life. The setting free of the slaves of Pharaoh becomes the setting free of the slaves of sin.[1]

The Cup in the Garden

After the Passover meal, Jesus went into the Garden of Gethsemane to pray, and the image of the cup recurred. Jesus went a little way ahead of his disciples, fell to his knees and prayed, "Abba, Father, all things are possible for you. Remove this cup from me. Yet not what I will, but what you will" (Mark

> *The cup was that future course offered by his Father.*

14:36). Luke records that Jesus was "in agony" and "he prayed more earnestly, and his sweat became like great drops of blood falling down to the ground" (Luke 22:44).

Within the story, the cup seemed to represent Jesus' destiny. Drinking the cup would mean accepting the path before him; refusing the cup would be resisting his calling and trying to turn aside from the direction God had given him. The cup was that future course offered to him by his Father.

We know that Jesus knew the Hebrew Scriptures. I wonder, as he prayed, if Jesus recalled any of the other Biblical uses of the *cup.* Surely, he knew by heart Psalm 16 in which David prays, "The LORD is my chosen portion and my cup." That measure that was allotted to David in life was nothing less than God himself. Jesus knew, too, of Psalm 23: "You anoint my head with oil; my

---

1   Lane, William; *The Gospel of Mark* (Grand Rapids, Mich.; William B. Eerdmans Publishing Company; 1974) pp. 504-513. Lane gives an excellent commentary on the relationship between the Passover and the Last Supper .

cup overflows." The cup represents one's very life, which can overflow with the presence of the LORD.

But the cup, also in the Old Testament, can symbolize the judgment of God. In Psalm 11, David declares that for the wicked, "fire and sulfur and a scorching wind shall be the portion of their cup." A just God who "loves righteous deeds" will set all things right. He will not allow arrogant oppressors to continue indefinitely. Psalm 75 goes further: "For in the hand of the LORD there is a cup with foaming wine, well mixed, and he pours out from it, and all the wicked of the earth shall drain it down to the dregs." Those who boastfully defy God will be made to drink the cup of his judgment. For the LORD will set right what has gone wrong. Moreover, when we read of the LORD disciplining his wayward people, the image of the cup is vivid. Psalm 60 laments: "You have made your people see hard things; you have given us wine to drink that makes us stagger." The King James Version translates it as "the wine of astonishment." The prophet Isaiah described it as, "you who have drunk from the hand of the LORD the cup of his wrath, who have drunk to the dregs the bowl, the cup of staggering" (Isaiah 51:17).

These passages evoke a cup bubbling over with destruction. What is given from the LORD is judgment for a rebellious people who had forgotten the poor and forgotten the LORD. Praying in the garden, Jesus associated the cup he was about to drink with *this* cup. At the supper, he understood the cup of judgment and redemption to be connected with the shedding of his blood. Now, in the garden, he recognized that the cup he would soon drink (i.e., the suffering he would undergo), would be the acceptance of judgment upon him that would lead to freedom for us. Though he desperately prayed to be spared the cup, he went on to consecrate himself to the task.

The Meaning of Wrath

Jesus was about to drink a cup of wrath. The idea of God's judgment is hard for us. We wonder why God displays such wrath in the Bible when our religion is supposed to be about a loving God. But there is no escaping it. From Genesis through Revelation, including the Psalms which we cherish and the words of Jesus we love, God judges human sin.

How are we to understand this cup of wrath before Jesus? It is helpful to me to consider that wrath is not a primary emotion, but a secondary one. Anger is the result of something else. Wrath may arise from offense. When one's sense of what is right is violated, anger occurs. Indignation at the unjust suffering of others quickens a righteous wrath. Moreover, wrath may be derived from pain, either feared or experienced, for oneself or for others. The very angry person often is a very pained one. Perhaps deeply scarred by a terrible wrong, or threatened by an uprooting change, or finding our children in harm's way,

Wrath can arise from love.

we may be roused to a ferocious anger. Wrath can be a reaction of protection, and even may be an expression of love when the loved one faces harm.

If we follow this reasoning a bit farther, we may probe what outrage at injustice God has undergone in dealing with the human race. Indeed, what pain has God known in his love for humanity that has kindled his wrath? What fierce passion of a holy God for his wayward children was poured into the goblet of wrath that Jesus drank?

I do not believe it merely was the pain caused when someone deducted a dubious business trip on a tax return. Nor is the goblet overfilled because someone let slip a swear word in traffic and another had a few too many at the Christmas party. We too easily can be full of our petty mistakes, hiding from God as from a headmaster who lives to catch students in menial sins.

But all the while, I am wrapped in my little worries. A boy looks with dismay and incomprehension as a parent walks out the door. "It's not your fault," he is told but, years later, he still believes it is. Children cry in hunger and others call the problem "politics," mumbling things such as, "Those people need to get a work ethic." Rain forests are bulldozed, while the waters are over-fished and fouled with sewage. The elderly are forgotten and the unborn no longer are safe in the womb. Terror finds ever new ways to shock us. The weak continue to be swindled by the strong. Life is louder and harsher every day. The whole world is out of tune. It's a mess.

For such pain in the world, even we are outraged. As narcissistic as I am most of the time, the suffering in the world still can move me to wrath. And if we get angry, do we not think that God, who loves so much more than we, also gets angry? The righteous wrath of God surely is kindled by the suffering we cause one another. Yet, we must note that this wrath of God is not like the outrage of a petty tyrant whose merest whim was denied. Our God is not easily offended. Rather, Scripture tells us that God is "slow to anger and abounding in steadfast love" (Psalm 103:8). God's everlasting love and absolute holiness are inseparable. Human sin offends his love. Injustice cries out to God's heart of mercy to be righted.

We tend to look at judgment only as a negative, but the wrath of God actually is good news. The fact that there is judgment in God means that sin and evil not always will have their way in the world. Things will not spin endlessly out of control. Rather, they will be set right. The kingdom of God will come. God's way will prevail on the earth as well as in heaven. In the full establishment of his justice, the creation will be restored to what it was intended to be.

The Man Who Drank The Cup Was God!

So, in the garden, there was a cup of wrath to be drunk. Jesus chose to drink it rather than decline the cup and let it be poured out onto the world as judgment. The cup he drank, taking wrath into himself, becomes for us the cup of blessing. The cup of judgment becomes the cup of salvation. This is what Jesus proclaimed at the Passover supper, chose in the garden, and endured in his death on the cross.

We only can understand this by recognizing a startling truth. Jesus was not just a guy. I mentioned this briefly in the introduction, and it has been intimated throughout this study through the extraordinary things we have seen Jesus say and do. But now, the truth can come out from under wraps. Jesus is the eternal Son of God who came to us as a man. When Jesus speaks and acts, he speaks and acts both as a man and as God. On the one hand, he is the *man* in our place, living out a life of obedience and faithfulness to his Father. The intimacy with God we could not know, Jesus lived out and, as he did so, he offered it to us. On the other hand, Jesus is *God* come among us. He gives his life, not just as a man taking the wrath of God, but also as God himself taking our place, acting on our behalf, solving the problem of human sin that we cannot solve.

> *The sacrifice of Jesus on the cross was an act of God himself.*

The sacrifice of Jesus on the cross was an act of God himself. The cup and the cross do not represent an angry God taking it out on the best man who ever lived. Rather, the cup and the cross represent God coming to stand in for us. God himself entered our world and drank down his own bowl of wrath against sin. He allowed our rejection of his love to nail him to the cross. In fact, he received in himself all the sins of the world and all the judgment due those sins. In the moment he cried out, "My God, why have you forsaken me?" (Mark 15:34), Jesus even entered the hell of our lostness. He underwent the agony that we deserved in being cut off from God. The drinking of the cup was enacted on the cross as the mightiest of the mighty acts of God. Wrapped in our flesh in Jesus, God himself drank his own just judgment on our sin. He accepted it in our place, deep within, to the point of death.

What The Cup Means for Us

This cup, the third cup of Passover, would now and forever be the sign of the new covenant, the new relationship between God and humanity, established and sealed in his blood. We return to the image with which we began this chapter. A great exchange has occurred. The cup of wrath becomes the cup of blessing. Jesus drank down the bitterness of sin and offers us the wine of salvation. The poet George Herbert said it well when he wrote: "Love is that liquor sweet and most divine/Which my God feels as blood but I as wine."[1]

Because Jesus has drunk the cup, we are free to face our lives. We are free to look at all the pain that has been inflicted upon us, and no longer be overwhelmed with debilitating shame. All the sickness that has diminished us, all the pathology that has damaged us, need no longer rule us.

And, in turn, we are free to face all the pain we have inflicted on others, and know that we may stop. We may receive grace. We may start anew. There is real forgiveness to be had. On that basis, we may begin to set things right.

Jesus has drunk the cup. We need no longer live under the wrath that leads to destruction and bitterness. We may give up the anger of our woundedness and the anger that covers over the guilt of the wounds we have given, for Jesus has drunk these down as his own. He has known trouble in his soul unto death, agony of decision unto sweating drops of blood, pain in his body beyond the limits of mortal enduring, and utter humiliation of his gracious offers of love. He has gone beyond where any of us have gone and, in so doing, has redeemed us from all sins committed by us and against us.

So, he declares that we may let our pain go. There is peace the other side of owning and giving over our rage to Jesus. There is healing the other side of owning and giving over our destructive ways of living to Christ. There is joy the other side of owning and giving over our guilt and bitterness and failure to him. We may pour it all into his cup. He will drink it. We can let it go. Someone has paid for all

---

1   Herbert, George; "Sacraments;" *The Complete English Poems*; Tobin, John; ed. (London; Penguin Books: 1991).

this trouble. Jesus has drunk the cup of the world's pain to the dregs. The cup of judgment has become the cup of redemption. So, we may join our voices to Psalm 116 and sing: "What shall I render to the LORD for all his benefits to me? I will lift up *the cup of salvation* and call on the name of the LORD." We toast the LORD God as at a festive banquet, lifting up the cup of celebration as a symbol of the salvation he so graciously has poured into our cups.

QUESTIONS FOR DISCUSSION AND REFLECTION

The story of the cup is found in Mark 14:22-42.

* What thoughts have you had about the apparent contradiction between the love of God and the wrath of God?
* How is Jesus' life and death God's answer to the pain of the world and the wrath of God?
* What is the connection between the death of Jesus and the forgiveness of sins?
* Jesus said in an act of consecration, "Nevertheless not my will but your will be done." How might that statement be applied to our life in Christ?
* What could it mean in your relationships to discover that Jesus already has suffered for the pain you both have experienced and caused?
* How does Christ's drinking of the cup affect your response to Jesus' assertion that those who would follow him must take up their cross and deny themselves?

Exercises

* Write down several memories, emotions or habits you wish could be put into Jesus' cup.
* Using rich colors from Crayola or markers, draw the cup that Jesus drank. Allow it to contain the mistakes, pain, sin, and suffering that you need to pour in at this time. Discuss with a partner or in a journal your reactions when you are finished. Perhaps offer this cup to Jesus in prayer.
* Practice this meditative exercise, preferably in a group setting. Use the opening paragraphs of this chapter to visualize meeting Jesus. Imagine yourself pouring in the emotions and the memories, the anger, shame, pain and guilt. See Jesus taking them from you in his cup, and drinking it down. Then hear him say as he passes the cup back, "This is my blood, which is poured out for you and for

many for the forgiveness of sins." See yourself drain the cup and feel its contents fill you. Visualize how Jesus then embraces you and sends you back into your daily life.

+ Debrief this exercise with a partner; make notes in a journal.

Chapter 11

BURNING HEARTS

Luke 24: 13-35

As we prepare to move to a story that occurred after Jesus' crucifixion, one final thought about the cup Jesus drank must first be explored. It is a hard one. Jesus expected that his followers also would drink his cup, not only of blessing, but also of suffering. He knew that whoever loved him would have to take a road that led through death to new life. For some of his early disciples, that meant a literal death under persecution. For all of us who come to be joined to Christ, it means a kind of dying to self, the end of an old way of living. Jesus said, "If anyone would come after me, let him deny himself and take up his cross and follow me. For whoever would save his life will lose it, but whoever loses his life for my sake and the gospel's will save it" (Mark 8:34-5).

As we saw earlier, Jesus promised James and John that they indeed would drink the *same cup* that he had to drink. Symbolically speaking, that cup extends to all of us who follow Jesus. We drink the cup of his blessing, taking in his forgiveness, acceptance and healing. We also drink the cup of his suffering. Not that we must experience the judgment of God on sin and the fearful separation from God of the cross – Jesus has done that for us once and for all. But we do share in his sufferings as we struggle against continuing sin in our lives or experience persecution for our faith in him.

> We also drink the cup of his suffering.

This is the way I hear his voice: "You, too, will suffer with me. You will lose yourselves if you are to be my followers. This is the way of the Kingdom. This is the essence of who I am and what I am doing here. I lay down my life from beginning to end in love."

"I am the healer; I am the binder of wounds; I am the forgiver of sins; I am the embracer of outcasts. I also am death. I am death to the life that does not belong to God. I am death to anything but living wholeheartedly for the sake of God's little ones. I go to my death. You must follow as you are required.

"This is the way of God. I must suffer and give my life for the ransom of many. I take your pain unto myself. I hug your diseases and make them whole. I bear your sins in my body as I hang on the cross. But more. Oh, more. I call you to go along the way I have walked. You are to live with the cross on your back. You will drink the cup I drink. If you would be mine, every day, every hour, devote your life to me; embrace these little ones who seem not to count. Every day, be the servant. Deny yourself for the sake of your Lord and his children."

Jesus understood his death as following inevitably upon his ministry. He knew his light would be too bright for most. Yet, he did not turn from his mission. What's more, he knew that his followers would be united to his death. Romans 6:3 tells us that "all of us who were baptized into Christ Jesus were baptized into his death." And, as the poet T.S. Eliot has noted, "The time of death is every moment."[1] Following Jesus is a moment-by-moment dying to self and living to and for Christ. Awakening to God through discovering Jesus truly does transform us. But new life means the death of the old. Christianity is a muscular, radical, complete commitment. We must have no illusions about our purpose. He calls us totally to himself.

> Christianity is a muscular, radical, complete commitment.

Called To New Life With Christ

Thankfully, though, as we are joined to Jesus, we are not left only in the garden or on the cross. Resurrection followed Jesus' death. The man who died on the cross was buried in a tomb, but on the third day he rose again from the dead. The Jesus who lived again was the *same* Jesus who had died. He spoke to his disciples. He ate with them. They knew him. But he also was *different*. His body was transformed. Though he bore the marks of the wounds from the nails and the spear, he was vivid with life. He was so real that even locked doors seemed insubstantial to him – he passed right through them. Jesus in resurrection became a man outfitted for life in heaven. He was himself, only more so. He was humanity without the curse of death and decay upon him. Eternal life coursed

---

1   Eliot, T. S.; "The Dry Salvages; *Four Quartets* (London; Faber and Faber; 1944) p. 36.

through him in body and spirit.

Jesus' disciples experienced that this resurrection life and power also could flow within them. Their bodies, of course, were not yet transformed. They still had to die, as we all do. But they had received what Jesus promised (John 14:16-17). He sent his Holy Spirit to dwell in their hearts. So, Jesus' life pulsed within them. This resurrection life of Jesus remains available to those who have shared the cup with him. So, dying with Jesus is part of our reconnecting with God. But it is not the whole story. What we lose in following Jesus, we quickly learn to call the *old* life, for he is constantly giving us *new* life. We can

> He is constantly giving us new life.

be linked with the resurrection of Jesus in such a way that our lives are recreated. It is possible to access the vivifying power of one who died and then lived again, for his Spirit comes to dwell within all who are joined to him by faith. Our next story helps us explore this reality.

On The Emmaus Road

On the Sunday evening after Jesus was crucified on the Friday before, two men were walking along the road from Jerusalem to Emmaus. A stranger joined then along the way. "What are you discussing?" he asked? They replied smartly, "Are you the only visitor to Jerusalem who doesn't know about the things that have happened in these days?"

The stranger played dumb. "What things?"

So, they told him about Jesus of Nazareth. "Once we thought he was the man who would redeem the nation. He was a miracle worker and a man who spoke the Word of God. Then the chief priests and the rulers condemned him to death. Turns out he was just another guy after all. Except that this morning some of our women reported that his tomb was empty. They said they saw angels who said he was alive. Some of our friends checked it out, and the body is indeed gone. But we can't figure it out."

Of course, they did not recognize that the stranger walking with them was actually Jesus himself. Luke tells us that their eyes were prevented from recognizing him: "Jesus said to them, 'O foolish ones and slow of heart to believe! Was it not necessary that Christ should suffer these things and enter into his glory?'" Then this "stranger" began with the books of Moses and worked his way forward through the Scriptures, interpreting all the passages that referred to the Messiah.

So, Jesus explained to them how the Hebrew Scriptures actually pointed to him (though they did not yet realize he was talking about himself). What would it have been like to have walked that seven-mile journey with Jesus teaching the meaning of those passages? In those priceless hours, Jesus unfolded the whole story of God's redemption. He unlocked the Word for his disciples. I wonder which Scriptures he chose to discuss. Can you imagine having Jesus himself explain to you the deepest meaning of the Bible and to show you passage by passage how he is the key to everything? As I imagine being part of this scene, I would love to have heard about:

> *Jesus unlocked the Word for his disciples.*

+ Genesis 3:15. The LORD God curses the serpent by saying there will be enmity between the serpent and the woman and her offspring. Concerning one of those offspring, the LORD tells the serpent, "He shall bruise your head and you shall bruise his heel." Did Jesus say that as a prophecy of the Messiah? Did Jesus come to crush the head of Satan through his resurrection, after the devil had struck his heel on the cross?

+ Genesis 22:2. The darkest and most troubling passage in the Hebrew Scriptures. The LORD God asks Abraham to sacrifice Isaac, the son of the Promise. The LORD demands that the long-awaited fulfillment of Abraham's hopes, given to him by the LORD, now be offered up like a sheep for sacrifice. At the last moment, the LORD stays Abraham's hand and provides a ram in the bushes for the sacrifice. Did Jesus explain that the episode was meant to show us how God so loved the world that he gave his only begotten Son for us? God provides the sacrifice, his own son for the world, so that we may go free.

+ Exodus 12:13. The final, horrible plague comes upon Egypt as the first-born are slain by the angel of death. But on the doors of the house of the Israelites was the blood of a pure lamb. The angel of death passed over those homes and spared the children. Then, in the morning, the people were set free. They passed through the parted waters of the Red Sea to safety. Did Jesus explain to his disciples that afternoon how he is the Lamb of God who takes away the sins of the world? He is our Passover. By him, we are spared judgment, and pass safely through the waters of death into eternal life. I wonder if they felt the echo with his words about the cup when, at the Last Supper, Jesus inserted himself as the meaning of the cup of judgment and redemption?

• Psalm 22 eerily describes a crucifixion, hundreds of years before the foul Roman method of execution was practiced. Did Jesus describe how the cry of dereliction in verse 1 – "My God, why have you forsaken me?" – was taken up by Christ on the cross? Did he mention verse 18, predicting that they would "divide my garments among them and cast lots for my clothes?" How the disciples' hearts would have burned to hear what they had just witnessed two days earlier!

• Isaiah 53:4-5. "Surely he has borne our griefs and carried our sorrows ... he was wounded for our transgressions; he was crushed for our iniquities." Did Jesus tell them how this prophecy was not about Israel the nation, but about the suffering servant of the Messiah, the LORD God who came himself to redeem his people?

• Psalm 16:10 declares: "You will not abandon my soul to Sheol or let your holy one see corruption." Did Jesus quote that passage just before he confirmed to them the Christ who was crucified would fulfill his own prediction and he would be raised from the dead?

Those are just a few passages he might have discussed. We see it so clearly now. But, then, the expectations were different. People expected a conquering Messiah, and that the Kingdom of God would come in one sudden triumph. Jesus had to show them how it always had been God's plan to come in person. He came first to suffer, then to triumph. Jesus showed them how he fulfilled the ancient prophecies.

Their Eyes Were Opened

They must have hung on his every word. When they reached the village, Jesus acted as if he would journey on, but they were desperate to stay with him. They pleaded with him to stop for supper and the night. The order for evening prayer in the Episcopal Church has a prayer based on this passage:

> Lord Jesus, stay with us, for evening is at hand and the day is past; be our companion in the way, kindle our hearts, and awaken hope, that we may know you as you are revealed in Scripture and the breaking of the bread.[1]

So, Jesus did stay with them. That night, at supper, Luke tells us that Jesus "took the bread and blessed it and broke it and gave it to them." The feeling of *déjà vu* must have been overwhelming. This is what had happened three nights before in the upper room when Jesus took the bread during the Passover meal, gave it to his disciples, and said, "This is my body, broken for you." In that moment, they got it. Their eyes were opened and they recognized Jesus. Immediately, he vanished from their sight.

The disciples turned to each other and said, "Were not our hearts burning within while he talked to us on the road, while he opened to us the Scriptures?" They got up and journeyed in the dark as fast as they could back to Jerusalem. They found the eleven. They burst in and were greeted with the news, "The Lord is risen indeed and has appeared to Simon!" Then, these two who had journeyed from Emmaus shared their story of how Jesus was made known to them in teaching the Scriptures and the breaking of the bread.

From this story, we can make at least four key applications to our lives:

1) This is an extraordinary story of how the Lord Jesus *ordinarily* makes himself known to us. He speaks to us through his Scriptures. He reveals himself through the re-enactment of his Last Supper . Luke tells us that Jesus was made known to them in the breaking of the bread. The Holy Spirit particularly uses our participation in the sacrament of communion to show us who Jesus is and unite us to himself at a deeper level. As the bread is broken and the cup is passed, we are joined to him and one another and our knowledge of Jesus deepens. Communion is literally eye-opening.

---

1   *The Book of Common Prayer* (San Francisco; Seabury/Harper Collins; 1979) p.124.

Of course, the sacraments always are linked to the Word of God. Jesus opened the Scriptures to the disciples. He enabled them to see the meaning in the words of Scripture. Without the work of the Spirit of Jesus, we might look right at Jesus and not see him for who he is. It's as if there is a veil over our eyes but, when the Spirit takes away the veil, we can see clearly.

Creating spiritual sight in our blind minds and hearts is equivalent to an act of creation! In 2 Corinthians 4, we read that God spoke his word and created light out of the darkness. Paul goes on to tell us that the same God who created light in the dark has shone his light into our hearts so that we might see who Jesus is. When we realize that the glory of God is shining in the face of Jesus, when we see that he is our Lord and Savior, it means that God has done a work of new creation in us.

> *Creating spiritual sight in our blind hearts is equivalent to an act of creation!*

This is why, in our church, we pray before we read Scripture. We ask for illumination. We pray that God would take the words off the page and make them living words shining in our hearts. We pray that we would know Jesus through his Word.

For me, as a 14 year-old yielding my life to Christ, I experienced this reality very dramatically. Paul wrote that when someone turns to the Lord, the veil is taken away. One day, I read the Bible and it seemed far removed from me, a word I could not understand, a word for someone else. The night after I invited Jesus into my heart, the Word came alive. It seemed to be written just for me. The change was dramatic and exhilarating. I know now that this is the work of the Holy Spirit in the heart. He opens the Word for us so that we can meet Jesus through it.

2) New Testament scholar Tom Wright has noted an important parallel between our story in Luke 24 and the account of humanity's fall in Genesis.[1] This connection, Wright says, shows that we are meant to understand that the resurrection of Jesus has significance all the way back to our creation. The resurrection of Jesus means a re-working of our very humanity, a restoration from the Fall.

The man and the woman in the Garden of Eden were in perfect harmony. They were naked and, yet, felt no shame – there was complete openness. But the moment after they ate the forbidden fruit, the text tells us, "Then the eyes of

---

1   Wright, N.T.; *The Resurrection of the Son of God* (Philadelphia; Fortress Press; 2003) p. 652.

both were opened, and they knew that they were naked. And they sewed some fig leaves together and made themselves loincloths" (Genesis 3:7). They ate the fruit and their eyes were open to shame. Innocence was lost. Their eyes were opened to ruin. We lost our ability to speak and walk with God face-to-face. The tree of life was chained away. We lost Paradise and were exiled to the land of thorns and toil, death and pain. Humanity seized the forbidden fruit and our eyes were opened to fearsome loss.

By contrast, the Lord Jesus obeyed his Father and drank the bitter cup of death on the cross. He offered to the disciples the fruit of his sacrifice, the bread that was broken on their behalf. When they haltingly took from his hand the bread, their eyes were opened and they saw Jesus for who he is. Our eyes were opened to glory. Now, we could meet with God again. Now, we could see the glory of God shining in the face of Jesus Christ. Now, Paradise was open to us again. The bitter fruit of the cross became the glorious fruit of eternal life, available to all who would partake.

> *Our eyes were opened to glory.*

3) Thirdly, let us consider that wonderful phrase, the burning heart. "Did not our hearts burn within us while he talked to us on the road, while he opened to us the Scriptures?" The burning heart is not, of course, the heartburn of eating the wrong thing! The heart, the inner core of us, burns when we are on the edge of discovery. For instance, we arrive home to find an envelope on the table with our name on it. Perhaps it is from the publisher, the university, or the company from which we have been longing to hear. As we open it, our hearts burn in anticipation. This is it! Or, finding the light blinking on the phone may mean that she has returned my call. My heart burns as I press the button to hear the message. Similarly, reading the name of the sender sends us tingling with anticipation to read the e-mail we were desperate to get. The hand may tremble on the handle of the door behind which lie answers we have sought. In the moment just before discovery, we feel the burning heart. This is my heart's desire coming to the surface. This is what I am looking for! This is what I've searched for all my life! For the disciples, their wildest dreams were coming true. The heart burned with the rise of recognition and expectation. As we awaken to God through discovering Jesus, the burning heart may well become a regular part of our lives. There is a thrill of discovery in reading the Scriptures. Once we have realized how much we are loved, our hearts reply with joy, just as they were created to respond. When we learn new wonders about this One who has called us, claimed us and forgiven us, our hearts sing. There is no end to the depths of

discovery we can make all through our lives, for God not only exists, he makes himself known to us. His nature, his very being, is love. He includes us in that love, just as he takes us into his very life.

The reality that the one God is three becomes no longer some mathematical puzzle to perplex academics. Rather, it reveals how we are included in an eternal love story. God has been revealed as our tender, loving, heavenly Father. We know this because the eternal Son came among us in Jesus Christ. He loved his Father, as he had from all eternity, though now he did it as a man among us. And he let us overhear the intimacy of this relationship. What's more, the Father and the Son desire us to partake of their love. The Holy Spirit comes to dwell in our hearts, uniting us to Christ and enabling us to live in the love of the one Triune God. When our minds and souls are open to this reality, we truly enter the realms of wonder.

4) Furthermore, the way the disciples recognized Jesus tells us how much we need each other. Ultimately, it is up to God to illumine the truth of the resurrection for us. Jesus is the one who lifted the fog from his followers' eyes. But the recognition came in the context of the disciples' conversation during their journey, of their considering together the Scriptures Jesus recited, and of their being together at the table.

> *In the moment just before discovery, we feel the burning heart.*

We need one another to help us recall the stories that set our hearts burning. Other people are necessary companions for discussing and processing all the events of our lives as we make our way along the road. We need each other to learn how to wield the signs and symbols of faith. We even need each other to help get us to church and study groups. Many aspects of reconnecting to God have to be done in solitude, but we never get very far without others to keep us going.

The Power of the Resurrection

The power of Jesus' resurrection for us lies in the fact that Jesus' followers are mystically linked both to his dying and his rising. We may access the great energy of Jesus' resurrection in our own lives. In his letter to the Ephesians, the Apostle Paul prayed for the believers in a way closely linked to the meaning of our story from Luke. His words soar like a great hymn of praise as he considers the reality that has been revealed by Jesus. The superlatives pile ever higher, for Paul wants the believers to get in on all the wonder of Christ. He prayed:

that the God of our Lord Jesus Christ, the Father of glory,
may give you a spirit of wisdom and of revelation in the knowledge
of him, having the eyes of your hearts enlightened,
that you may know what is the hope to which he has called you,
what are the riches of his glorious inheritance in the saints,
and what is the immeasurable greatness of his power toward us
who believe, according to the working of his great might that he
worked in Christ
when he raised him from the dead and
seated him at his right hand in the heavenly places,
far above all rule and authority and power and dominion,
and above every name that is named,
not only in this age but also in the one to come.

Ephesians 1:17-21

The greatness of his power in us is commensurate with the same power by which the Father raised Jesus from the dead. That is why Paul could go on to say that, though we once "were dead in our trespasses, [now God] has made us alive together with Christ." He has "raised us up with [Christ] and seated us with him in the heavenly places" (Ephesians 2:5-6). Before we were joined to Jesus, we were dead in the water, spiritually speaking. Our sins separated us from our Father. But in Christ, we have been joined to his death so that the guilt of our sins died, as it were, with Christ on the cross. Now, too, we have been raised with Christ. We have the new life of his Spirit within us. The true location of our lives is in heaven with Christ. That is our home and our deepest identity.

> We have been raised with Christ!

Morton Kelsey has written: "Since Jesus has risen from the dead, there is no power which he cannot overcome."[1] The forces of evil and sin in the world ripped Jesus away from us on the cross. They did their worst, and it killed him. But those powers were not stronger than the life of God. In his resurrection, Jesus was given back to us and nothing, no power, can separate us from him now. We are his forever, kept by the power of his rising.

In terms of daily life, we draw on this resurrection power. Throughout this study, we have explored the great energy for life that Jesus had. His stories

---

1   Kelsey, Morton; *Dreams* (New York; Paulist Press; 1978) p. 40.

118

revealed the resurrecting quality of God's all-forgiving love for us. The father told the prodigal, "This son of mine was dead and is alive again; he was lost and is found!" In his personal encounters, Jesus offered the clarity of living water to the woman at the well, and a new start to the weeping woman plagued by her past. He had the strength to show a deeper way to the rich man, and the courage to bend down to wash his disciples' feet. In all his interactions, Jesus offered to free people from their old, lifeless ways and to guide them into the vivid life of following him. The beginning always meant a kind of death; the ending, for those who passed through the first stage, always meant a kind of resurrection.

By now, I am hopeful that you number yourself as one of Jesus' followers, for true life, eternal life, means being joined to Jesus' death and resurrection. We have a fresh start in Christ. Even more, the Spirit of Jesus now lives within us. We have risen with Christ. This is our heritage as Christians. This is our present reality in day-to-day living. This is our future hope. We may claim it, lean upon it, and revel in it at any time.

QUESTIONS FOR REFLECTION AND DISCUSSION

The story of the disciples' walk to Emmaus is found in Luke 24:13-35.

+ What questions or difficulties have you had about the resurrection?
+ What would you have liked to talk to Jesus about as he explained the Scriptures?
+ What do you imagine kept the disciples from recognizing Jesus?
+ Why do you suppose the breaking of the bread brought the moment of illumination for them?
+ What do you think the disciples meant when they said, "Did not our hearts burn within us while he talked to us on the road, while he opened to us the Scriptures?"
+ What does the phrase "burning heart" evoke for you? When have you felt this burning in your innermost person? What followed the sensation?
+ What moments of resurrection have you known in your life? Have there been any turning points in really believing in Jesus' resurrection?
+ What difference does it make in situations you face to know that you have the same power – the indwelling Holy Spirit – that made Jesus available to you? How do we access such power?

Exercises

- Individually, work on a dialogue in which you join the other two disciples along the road to Emmaus and speak to Jesus about his life, death and resurrection. Allow your questions to surface, and allow his replies to arise through answers or actions.
- If you are working with a group, and after writing the dialogues, hold a group dialogue in which you discuss the meaning of Jesus' resurrection, your experiences of resurrection, and any insights you gained from your writing.
- Consider a situation in which you are having difficulty. Imagine what it means to die with Christ in this situation; i.e., by putting his will first. Imagine what it means to be risen with Christ in this situation. Invite his resurrection power to enter this difficulty and transform it.

Chapter 12

HEARTFELT

John 21:1-15

Our final story took place after the resurrection. Though Jesus had met them along the road to Emmaus and in other places, he had not remained steadily with the disciples. Perhaps, then, they were unclear about what to do next.

At the beginning of John 21, Simon Peter decided to go back to doing what he knew how to do. He and some of the others went fishing. Once before they had fished all night and caught nothing, until Jesus sent them out for the miraculous catch. This night was the same, for their fishing had left them empty-handed. At dawn, they saw a man standing on the beach. He called to them, "Children, do you have any fish?" When they replied that they did not, he suggested, "Cast the net on the right side of the boat, and you will find some." They cast it as he suggested and, suddenly, there were so many fish that they could not haul the net aboard.

A flash of *deja vu* went through John: "It is the Lord!" Instantly, Simon Peter also realized that the man on the shore was the resurrected Jesus. Without hesitation, he "threw himself into the sea" and swam for the beach. The others followed in the boat.

Jesus was cooking fish and bread over a charcoal fire. He asked the disciples to add some of their fish to the feast. When the food was ready, he said, "Come and have breakfast." Then, Jesus "took the bread and gave it to them, and so with the fish." Again, the feeling of *deja vu* passed through them. Here was the Last Supper and the dinner in Emmaus all over again. Jesus kept making himself known to them. Whenever Jesus broke bread and shared it, they knew him in a deeper way. They were joined to him even as they recognized that he was their Lord. So, in that rather odd setting, the disciples ate breakfast with their master who had returned from the dead.

After breakfast, Jesus turned to Simon Peter. "Simon son of John, do you love me more than these?"

Simon immediately replied, "Yes, Lord; you know that I love you."

And, just as quickly, Jesus added, "Feed my lambs."

Then he asked Peter again, "Simon, son of John, do you love me?" Once more, Simon Peter affirmed his reply. "You know that I love you."

So, Jesus told him, "Tend my sheep."

Then, Jesus asked still another time, "Simon, son of John, do you love me?"

The text tells us that Simon was grieved that Jesus had to keep asking. He answered emphatically, "Lord, you know everything; you know that I love you."

And Jesus simply said, "Feed my sheep."

We have seen the use of repetition in the story of the washing of the feet and in the parable of the sheep and goats. Once again, the importance Jesus placed on his question is unmistakable. He wanted much more than a casual, immediate response. Jesus required Simon Peter to answer from his depths. The most apparent reason for the repetition is that Peter had denied knowing Jesus three times on the night before the crucifixion. Here was an opportunity for Peter to proclaim his love three times and so be restored. But, perhaps, there is even more to it, some dimension that affects us as well.

> *Do you love me more than these?*

Do You Love Me?

"Do you love Jesus?" The question is so straightforward as to be unnerving. One might reply, "Well, I don't know. I mean, I guess so. I don't *not* love Jesus. I want to follow him. Sure, all right, then, I love him." The first time the issue is raised, we might be able to stumble through and then forget about it.

> *He will not accept a superficial answer … it has to mean everything.*

But what if Jesus himself were to ask the question the second time, and call us by name when he asked, "Do you love me?" We might begin to get uncomfortable. Is there something the matter? Don't you believe me when I say I love you? You are making me doubt myself. I feel embarrassed.

And if he were to ask the question still a third time, we might realize how earnestly he desires our reply. He really does hope we will be bold enough to express our love. But he will not accept a superficial answer. It has to come from deep within; it has to mean everything. He is demanding that we become conscious of our disposition toward him. Simply plodding along not thinking about him will not do. He asks until we are awake enough to make a true answer. Jesus is relentless in this questioning and, behind his queries, is his love for us that is equally relentless. He loves us ardently. He has a work for us to do in the world. He wants to know our response.

How would you reply? The answer could be, "I don't know right now. I am not sure I know enough yet." But then, because Jesus keeps asking, you would have to consider how to express such ambivalence. Do you want to say, "No, I don't love you. I do not, I will not, love Jesus?" But if you were bold enough to articulate such a reply, then his repeated asking would force you to consider if that is truly the direction you want your life to take. Will you consciously live with the choice of not loving him?

By contrast, do you want to say, "Yes, of course I love you?" Or, if that is too bold for a hesitant faith, do you *want* to want to love Jesus? Is there some kernel, some tiny, irreducible part of you that is yearning to love Christ and express that love? If so, Jesus' questions will push you to consider how you can work with that spark of affection and fan it into a more ardent love.

An Evening of Discovery

Years ago, a great scientist had the experience of coming to terms with the reality of Jesus and the response required of him. Blaise Pascal was a French mathematician who lived in the 17th century. Pascal was the first scientist to prove the existence of a vacuum and also invented, among other things, the adding machine.

Exposed to the Christian faith, Pascal was yearning for a deeper connection with Christ. He knew the Scriptures, but had not yet had his eyes opened to their truth. Then, at the age of 31, Pascal had a visionary experience while reading John 17. There, in a little room in his house, Christ invaded his life. For two hours, it seemed that the very room was on fire. Pascal scrawled his thoughts on a piece of paper, along with a picture of a cross with rays beaming out of it. He sewed the paper into his vest pocket and, thus, carried it with him wherever he went. It was found after his death, which occurred eight years later. This is what he wrote:

The year of grace 1654,
Monday, 23 November. ...
From about half-past-ten in the evening until half past midnight
FIRE
'God of Abraham, God of Isaac, God of Jacob,'
     not of philosophers and scholars,
Certainty, certainty, heartfelt, joy, peace.
God of Jesus Christ.
God of Jesus Christ.
"My God and your God."
"Thy God shall be my God."
The world forgotten, and everything except God.
He can only be found by the ways taught in the Gospels.
Greatness of the human soul.
"O righteous Father the world had not known thee, but I have
known thee.'
Joy, joy, joy, tears of joy.
I have cut myself off from him.
"They have forsaken me, the fountain of living waters."
My God wilt thou forsake me?
Let me be not cut off from him forever!
"And this is life eternal, that they may know thee,
The only true God and Jesus Christ whom thou has sent."
Jesus Christ.
Jesus Christ.[1]

Pascal's heart burned with recognition. At last, he saw the truth. He surrendered his life to Jesus Christ. The true God is not the speculative, abstract "god of philosophers and scholars," but the God of Abraham. This is the God who made himself known in the real world of dust and swiftly passing time. He spoke to our forefathers but, in the fullness of time, he came himself to us in Jesus Christ. This by no means was an anti-intellectual experience. Pascal's mind was satisfied as never before. He was taken to the depths of the mind deeper than he had known before. His experience involved heart, mind, body and soul. There was

---

1   Pascal, Blaise; in *The Oxford Book of Prayer*; Appleton, George; ed. (Oxford; Oxford University Press; 1985) pp. 264-5.

no more compartmentalizing but, rather, a glorious sense of wholeness.

The reality of this God who revealed himself in Christ came to Pascal in sentences from Scripture, especially from John's gospel. The resurrected Jesus told Mary, "Go to my brothers and say to them, 'I am ascending to my Father and your Father, *to my God and your God*" (John 20:17). Jesus' relationship of intimacy with his Father could now belong to his disciples. Jesus' God became their God. And, in the great prayer recorded in John 17, Jesus said, "And this is eternal life, that they know you, the only true God, and Jesus Christ whom you have sent" (John 17: 3).

In Jesus, Pascal understood, he could be reconnected in loving intimacy to the "only true God." The fire of illumination burned in his mind. Doubt became certainty. Emptiness became heartfelt joy.

If you have not done so already, I invite you to read this quotation from Pascal aloud several times. Through it, I can feel a great sense of discovery, the kind of burning heart we studied in the last chapter. As Pascal discerned the reality of God, his love was awakened. All his studies had been fascinating, but were not a sufficient end in themselves. His brilliant, rational mind expanded to include the perception of his heart.

> *Christ invaded his life … Pascal was taken to depths deeper than he had known before.*

What he knew now was more than rational. "Certainty, certainty, *heartfelt*, joy, peace." Pascal's response to what God had revealed to him arose from the center of his soul.

Though You Have Not Seen Him

I imagine that his encounter with Jesus on the beach had a lasting effect on Simon Peter. As we noted, Jesus' three-fold questioning of his love gave Peter a chance to affirm his devotion to Jesus three times before others. This, in effect, undid the terrible three denials of even knowing Jesus that Peter made shortly after the Last Supper (Mark 14:66-72). Jesus restored Simon Peter to fellowship with him. We saw in our study of Luke 5, and the great catch of fish, that Jesus replied to Simon Peter's confession of unworthiness with a commission to join Jesus in becoming a fisher of people. Now, Jesus commissioned Peter again. He called upon him to care for

> *Vocalizing his love created assurance.*

his lambs – all those who would become believers. Vocalizing his love for his Lord created an assurance in Simon Peter that his heart again was true.

We can hear echoes of this scene as we read a letter Peter wrote years later. He was encouraging young disciples in their relationship with Jesus: "Though you have not seen him, you love him. Though you do not now see him, you believe in him and rejoice with joy that is inexpressible and filled with glory, obtaining the outcome of your faith, the salvation of your souls" (I Peter 1:8-9). Peter called forth their love by assuring them they already had the devotion they desired. He wrote to people he quite possibly had never met and told them that they loved Jesus and believed in him.

Could such assurance possibly be effective?

I remember the afternoon I read this passage and wondered, "Peter, how do you know that *I* love Jesus? You don't know anything about me. I don't even know myself if I love Christ or not." And then, as if in direct response to my unspoken question, these words of Simon Peter seemed to lift me out of myself and into the truth. I suddenly felt that I did not need to keep questioning myself about whether I felt enough or believed strongly enough, or was at the right place spiritually. I did not have to try to reconnect with God. There was nothing to search for. The words of this passage brought me to the place I had longed to be.

> *All I had to do was agree with what was declared about me.*

A wave of relief hit me. "All right," I thought. "I do love him. I don't have to pick at these introspective worries any more. Peter says I believe and I'll agree with that. I do believe. I really do love Jesus. I am, by God's grace, already connected."

There followed, as Pascal said, "an indescribable and glorious joy." Certainty came – heartfelt, and by grace not merit. Closeness, not by my striving, but as a gift. All I had to do was agree with what was declared about me. Though I have not seen him, I love him. Though you have not seen him, *you* love him. Though you do not see him now, you believe in him and you are obtaining the outcome of your faith, the salvation of your souls.

This experience, I now know, was the work of the blessed Holy Spirit. In Acts, we have the record of a sermon Peter preached on the day of Pentecost. We noted in the last chapter that Jesus had promised he would send the Holy Spirit to his disciples. By the Spirit, Jesus would dwell within them. They would be taken into the love of the Father and the Son by means of the Spirit. The Holy Spirit is the bond, the personal glue, between us and Christ, and the very bond of love between the Father and the Son. He is the great joiner. It is not necessary to understand the mathematics of how the one God is the three persons of the Father, Son and Holy Spirit. We apprehend first the truth of the Triune God as we are brought into an intimate relationship with him. Through Jesus, we get reconnected to his Father. We later discover that this life-changing relationship occurs only because God the Holy Spirit has worked inside us. You may read more about this in the Afterword, including some prayers you may make to ask that you be joined to Christ so he can live in your heart by the Holy Spirit.

For now, we note that we have recorded in the book of Acts the day Jesus kept his promise to send the Spirit. About a week after the resurrected Jesus returned to heaven, the disciples were gathered in a room praying. Suddenly, the room shook with a mighty wind. Tongues of fire rested on them and they began speaking the praises of God in other languages. A great crowd of people from all over the known world was in Jerusalem for the festival. The people marveled to hear their own languages spoken, and they asked what had happened. Peter rose to explain and to tell them about Jesus. In his sermon, he said, "This

> *Actually, it's about God's discovering us!*

Jesus God raised up, and of that we all are witnesses. Being therefore exalted to the right hand of God, and having received from the Father the promise of the Holy Spirit, he has poured out this that you yourselves are seeing and hearing" (Acts 2: 2-3). Peter told them how the Spirit was the gift from the Father through his Son Jesus to join people in their love.

When the people heard Peter's testimony, they begged him to tell them what to do. So, he replied succinctly, "Repent and be baptized every one of you in the name of Jesus Christ for the forgiveness of your sins, and you will receive the gift of the Holy Spirit" (Acts 2:38). We see a wonderful, mysterious dynamic at work. The Spirit creates opportunities for us to hear about Jesus. He opens our eyes so that we may see that Jesus is Lord and Savior. He summons us to believe and to put our lives in Christ's hands. We give our whole hearts but, even as we do so, we realize that it is the blessed Spirit of Jesus who is enabling us to do so.

As we reach the end of these pages of *Discovering Jesus: Awakening To God*, we realize that actually it's all about God's discovering us! He came looking for us in Jesus Christ. He found us in our brokenness and lostness. He gave us purpose, even in the midst of our failures. He drank the cup of judgment so that he might offer us the cup of blessing. He rose from the dead so that he now can give us new life. The Christian faith is really all about discovering how ardently we are sought. Reconnecting with God is about getting found. In the end, God's seeking, searching grace in Christ is the heart of everything.

Here, then, is communion deeper than we could can have imagined. Here is joy that not only survives suffering, but flourishes in it. Here is faith that gets tempered, refined and proven as it interacts with the world. Though we may be ridiculed or ignored, called crazy or fanatical for holding to this truth, we do not falter – for we love him. Once we have been found by God in Christ, we cannot help but believe in him. We know him because his Spirit is within us. There is within us a joy inexpressible and full of glory. By faith, we may let this joy rise through us to bless and season all we do. No wonder Peter wrote so passionately: "Blessed be the God and Father of our Lord Jesus Christ!" (I Peter 1:3).

Feed My Lambs

Finally, as we conclude, we come back around to the mission that Jesus gave to Simon Peter. Each time that Peter answered Jesus in the affirmative, Christ responded, "Feed my lambs. Tend my sheep." Jesus wanted Peter to experience and express confidence in his devotion, but that was not to be the end of it. The internal "Yes" required an outer expression. Peter's life was not just about the discovery of his own fulfillment in a relationship with Christ. There was work to be done. The lambs needed to be fed and the sheep tended.

We begin the journey of reconnecting to God because of our own needs. We find ourselves penniless and far from home, and our hunger sends us on the way. We find ourselves so thirsty that we finally have to ask for a drink when our water supply no longer satisfies. Our accumulation of wealth does not fulfill us and, before we know it, we are asking, "What must I do to inherit eternal life?" The weight of life can steal upon us so quickly that even before we know it, we are weeping at Jesus' feet. Our first steps arise out of our need, and that is perfectly fine. We were made to be in a relationship with our heavenly Father. Reconnecting is the necessary beginning point of our new lives.

But in the larger purposes of God, we do not follow Jesus just for our sakes. God wants to bring to the whole creation the healing love that Jesus gave to people. And for some unfathomable reason, God has chosen us human beings to be the heralds of that love. Others are waiting for us to reconnect with God so that we may bring the Father's tender mercies to them.

If this were just about my spiritual comfort or lack of it, I could justify piddling around for years. "I'll be miserable if I want to be, thank you very much."

But the heart of God is aching for our return. And the little ones whom Jesus loved so much are waiting for us to go to them. He sends us to wash feet and to care for the least of these. For our sake, and also for the sake of those to whom we are sent, we need to follow Jesus.

At the end of this study, I find that the query of Jesus still is piercingly clear: "Do you love me more than these?" More than all the other ways you have tried living? More than all the distractions you cherish? More than all the other paths you have taken? And sometimes, even in spite of myself, his Spirit cries out with my own soul, "Lord you know that I love you!" The response is more than rational; it is heartfelt. And, so, Christ's call is clarion: "Then feed my lambs."

QUESTIONS FOR REFLECTION AND DISCUSSION

The story of the breakfast on the beach is in John 21:1-19.

+ Why might Simon Peter have gone fishing that night? In what ways do we try to go back to our familiar lives after we have experienced a taste of the resurrection? What happens?
+ What do you imagine Simon Peter felt when Jesus first asked him the question, "Do you love me?" How about the second and third times?
+ How would you respond if Jesus asked you if you loved him?
+ How does it feel to you to try on Peter's affirmation "Though you have not seen him, you love him. Though you do not now see him, you believe in him?"
+ If faith in Jesus is ultimately a gift of the Holy Spirit, what, then, is our part?
+ Who are the lambs and sheep you suspect Jesus may want you to tend and feed?

Exercises

+ Pretend that you are Simon Peter later that night, reflecting on what happened on the beach. Write a paragraph expressing what you think Jesus was after by his questions, what you think he may want you to do, and how you are feeling since the encounter.
+ Spend an entire day assuming that you do believe in Jesus, that you do love him enough to want to follow him, and that you will feed his sheep. For the whole day, pretending if you need to, verbalize that affirmation and live as if it were so. In the evening, write a reflection on how it felt to assume such a

connection with God.

+ On the next day, reflect on whether your "trying on" of that relationship enabled you in any way to realize that you already are connected with God?

+ Read the brief Afterword that follows this chapter and consider if you can make that prayer your own.

Afterword

How to Reconnect with God
Through Being Joined to Jesus

In this book, I have tried to convey to you some of what I have seen and heard about Jesus in the Scriptures. I have tried to share what I know in my experience to be true. This is the bottom line: *You can awaken to God through discovering Jesus.* You can, indeed, come home to God. Living water, healing forgiveness, eternal life, a festive celebration of love – are all available. Jesus is the means and the way back to God his Father. I have met him through the pages of Scripture. But more so, I feel his presence in my heart even as I write. I know what it is to be joined to Jesus. He comes to dwell in those who trust in him by sending his Holy Spirit into our hearts. This is a soul-joining, a fellowship, in the deepest levels. It has meant the filling of loneliness, the assuaging of guilt, the thrill of purpose, companionship in suffering, entering a fellowship of compassion for the least and the lost, and the gift of an unflagging hope even in this lost, chaotic world.

I know Jesus because someone told me about him. People who had experienced his living presence passed Christ along. This is how it has been from the beginning. This is the way God reconnects us to himself. The first disciples wrote about what "we looked upon and have touched with our hands, concerning the word of life" (I John 1:1). They heard the sound of Jesus' voice. They knew his embrace. They saw him alive from the dead.

> *Today, we may be as close to Jesus as were his first followers!*

They were the witnesses that Jesus had come from God to reconnect us to God. As they told the story, these disciples discovered that even people who had never seen Jesus face-to-face came to know him in the same deep, transforming way that they did. As the disciples shared Jesus, others were united to him, just as if they, too, had known Jesus in the flesh.

So, we read: "That which we have seen and heard we proclaim also to you, so that you too may have fellowship with us; and indeed our fellowship is with the Father and his Son Jesus Christ" (I John 1:3). Distance and time are no barriers. Today, we may be as close to Jesus as were his first followers! We may enter the fellowship – the intimate, loving relationship – that Jesus shares with his Father.

How can this be so? Such present, vital union is a deep mystery. Jesus himself said it occurs through his gift to us of the Holy Spirit in our hearts. The Spirit joins us to Jesus. The Spirit is the bond of love, the spiritual glue, between Jesus and his Father, and between Jesus and his followers. By the Spirit, we come to be *in* Christ and he in us. Thus, we are joined to his own relationship and intimacy with his Father. All that he is and has become is ours as we are joined to him.

I cannot make you believe that Jesus is the Savior who will reconnect you to God his Father. In fact, you cannot make yourself believe it. *Faith is a gift.* It is the work of the Holy Spirit to awaken us to say "Yes" when we hear the stories of Jesus. *But faith also is a choice.* When the Spirit rouses my heart at hearing of Jesus, I am called to say with my whole heart, "Lord, I believe. Help my unbelief! Jesus, you are my Savior and the Lord of all. Jesus, you are the way to the Father. Jesus, I believe that your death takes away my sins. Your resurrection opens up eternal life to me. Jesus, I want you to live in me."

The question, then, at the end of this book and the end of the day is simply this: Is the Holy Spirit creating faith in you *right now?* Do you want to be reconnected to God through Jesus? If the Holy Spirit is stirring your spirit, I urge you not to wait another moment. Enter the fellowship. Experience the mystic communion of knowing God the Father through Jesus his Son in the loving bond of the blessed Holy Spirit. Add your agreement in heart, mind and will to what Christ has done for you and is doing for you.

> Is the Holy Spirit creating faith in you right now?

In Revelation 3: 20, Jesus used the image of knocking at the door and waiting for us to invite him in. He said, "Behold, I stand at the door and knock. If anyone hears my voice and opens the door, I will come in to him, and eat with him, and he with me." Opening the door is an act of faith. We invite Jesus to come into our hearts. We invite him to be Lord of our lives. We invite him to be our Savior. We invite him to reconnect us with his Father. We invite him to lead us in the way of loving and living as he did.

All that belongs to Jesus may be ours – his forgiveness, his mercy, his peace, his joy, his love. He knocks at the door and yearns for admittance. Don't wait another second! Invite him in right now. Here is a prayer you may use:

Lord Jesus, come into my heart. I have been the prodigal child and need your acceptance. I have been the judgmental older brother and need your joy. I have been the thirsty woman at the noonday well and I need your living water. I have wounds from the past that need your healing.

I admit that I have sought for good in bad, broken places. I have looked for life amidst what only makes for death. I have tried to hold on to what little I have because I fear that you will not be as good and loving as I need. Forgive me.

I desire eternal life and am willing to give up control of my earthly life to you. Come into my heart. All I have is yours. By faith, I accept that all that you are and have is mine. I receive the cup of your forgiveness because I know you drank the cup of my sin on the cross. I receive the joy of your resurrection life that has overcome all death. Set my heart burning with passion for you. Make me wholeheartedly willing and able from now on to serve you and love you and others all my days. Make me one who will wash the feet of others and care for even the least and the lost. Amen.

If that is indeed your prayer, I urge you as soon as possible to tell someone who is a Christian about the choice you made. Make plans to attend worship this Sunday. Seek a small group of people with whom you can study Scripture and pray. Read the Bible today and each day. (Psalms and the gospels make great places to start).

You have begun a great adventure. The Holy Spirit dwells in your heart. You are in Christ, forever joined to him. You belong to the Father and can never be taken from him. Eternal life has begun!

About the Author

Gerrit Scott Dawson is senior pastor of First Presbyterian Church in Baton Rouge, Louisiana, and previously served churches in Delaware and North Carolina.

He received a Bachelor of Arts degree with honors in English from Vanderbilt University, a Master of Divinity degree from Princeton Theological Seminary and a Doctor of Ministry degree from Reformed Theological Seminary in Charlotte, N.C.

Actively involved in seminar and retreat leadership, Dawson also has cultivated a writing ministry that includes, with Steve Strickler, *Living Stories*, an elementary Sunday school curriculum based on 125 core Bible stories; numerous articles for *Weavings: A Journal of the Christian Spiritual Life*; and a contribution to the spiritual formation program *Companions in Christ*.

He also is the author or editor of the following books:

Discovering the Incarnate Savior: An Introduction to Torrance Theology (forthcoming).

Given and Sent in One Love: The True Church of Jesus Christ (with Mark Patterson).

Jesus Ascended: The Meaning of Christ's Continuing Incarnation.

I Am With You Always: Meeting Jesus in Every Season of Life.

A Passion for Christ: The Vision that Ignites Ministry – Thomas Torrance, James B. Torrance and David W. Torrance (with Jock Stein).

Love Bade Me Welcome: Daily Readings with George Herbert.

Called by a New Name: Becoming What God Has Promised.

Writing on the Heart: Inviting Scripture to Shape Daily Life.

Heartfelt: Finding Our Way Back to God.

He and his wife, Rhonda, have four children: Micah, Leah, Jacob and Mary-Emeline.

Printed in the United States
70300LV00001B/139-393